Redash v5 Quick Start Guide

Create and share interactive dashboards using Redash

Alexander Leibzon
Yael Leibzon

BIRMINGHAM - MUMBAI

Redash v5 Quick Start Guide

Commissioning Editor: Sunith Shetty
Acquisition Editor: Siddharth Mandal
Content Development Editor: Kirk Dsouza
Technical Editor: Jinesh Topiwala
Copy Editor: Safis Editing
Project Coordinator: Hardik Bhinde
Proofreader: Safis Editing
Indexer: Rekha Nair
Graphics: Jason Monteiro
Production Coordinator: Shantanu Zagade

First published: September 2018

Production reference: 1290918

Published by Packt Publishing Ltd.
Livery Place
35 Livery Street
Birmingham
B3 2PB, UK.

ISBN 978-1-78899-616-7

www.packtpub.com

`mapt.io`

Mapt is an online digital library that gives you full access to over 5,000 books and videos, as well as industry leading tools to help you plan your personal development and advance your career. For more information, please visit our website.

Why subscribe?

- Spend less time learning and more time coding with practical eBooks and Videos from over 4,000 industry professionals

- Improve your learning with Skill Plans built especially for you

- Get a free eBook or video every month

- Mapt is fully searchable

- Copy and paste, print, and bookmark content

PacktPub.com

Did you know that Packt offers eBook versions of every book published, with PDF and ePub files available? You can upgrade to the eBook version at `www.PacktPub.com` and as a print book customer, you are entitled to a discount on the eBook copy. Get in touch with us at `service@packtpub.com` for more details.

At `www.PacktPub.com`, you can also read a collection of free technical articles, sign up for a range of free newsletters, and receive exclusive discounts and offers on Packt books and eBooks.

Foreword

It's amazing to realize that Redash started five years ago. It started as a hackathon project, which was open sourced two months later. I remember getting excited about the first 5 companies that started using Redash.

Today, Redash is a company on its own, and there are over 4500 teams around the world using Redash, both the open source project and the SaaS service. Reading the first book on Redash is another important milestone in Redash's maturity.

Alexander and Yael are great candidates to write the book. Alexander contributed code to the project and is very familiar with its internals, while Yael used it in various data projects for multiple companies since the early days of Redash.

I hope you will find this book useful, and it will help you start using Redash. You should also remember that Redash is an active open source project, which means it keeps evolving constantly. I suggest that you familiarize yourself with the knowledge base along with the active community. Happy querying!

Arik Fraimovich,
Redash Creator/Founder

Contributors

About the authors

Alexander Leibzon is a software infrastructure consultant and backend software developer with over 15 years' experience in the software development industry.

Alexander is a contributor to Redash and several other open source projects.

Prior to becoming an independent consultant, Alexander was a data infrastructure engineer at EverythingMe, the company where Redash was initially developed during a hackathon.

Alexander holds a BSc degree in physics and computer science.

I would like to thank my wife Yael, and kids for their patience and support throughout the writing process of the book, Arik for creating Redash, Kirk for keeping me on track with the schedule, and Tal for very helpful reviews.

Yael Leibzon is a data analyst with 8 years' experience in the industry. Yael has been an extensive user of Redash for over 3 years.

Yael holds an MSc in biomedical engineering. During Yael's academic research , Yael developed finite element computational models, which were published in biomedical literature.

I would like to thank my husband, Alexander, for giving me the opportunity to write this book with him and for his enormous support and never-ending motivation. I would like to thank my children for keeping me happy through tough deadlines. Finally, I'd like to thank the Packt publishing team and reviewers of this book.

About the reviewer

Arik Fraimovich created Redash as a hackathon project while working for EverythingMe in 2013. He founded the Redash company in 2015 to make sure Redash has a sustainable future. Arik is also a developer and entrepreneur, developing software professionally for over 15 years and has passion for solving real users' problems.

Tal Maizels is a chief technology officer with extensive experience in the marketing and advertising industry. Tal has led projects and teams in start-ups for the last 10 years in the fields of EdTech, consumer networks, and finance. An IT professional with a BSc in computer science and mathematics from Bar-Ilan University, Tal has over 20 years' experience in software development, design, and management, and is skilled in mobile applications, Java, **Software as a Service (SaaS)**, Continuous Integration, and Scrum.

Packt is searching for authors like you

If you're interested in becoming an author for Packt, please visit `authors.packtpub.com` and apply today. We have worked with thousands of developers and tech professionals, just like you, to help them share their insight with the global tech community. You can make a general application, apply for a specific hot topic that we are recruiting an author for, or submit your own idea.

Table of Contents

Preface

Redash is a relatively new player in the data querying and visualization ecosystem, yet it gains solid recognition levels as time passes by.

Redash was initially developed by developers who work with data to serve everyone who works with data. This concept remains the core of Redash, and the book's aims to expose that concept to the readers.

Who this book is for

The Book is for anyone who works with data, but it will best suit mixed data teams. Mixed means you have a developer, an analyst (optionally DBA/IT), and product. Those teams will benefit from all of Redash's features.

This book is intended for novices to intermediate-level Data Analysts and Developers.

Although as prior knowledge – nothing is really required, to get the most of the book you need to be fairly familiar with SQL syntax, as some linux knowledge is a great advantage.

What this book covers

Chapter 1, *Introducing Redash*, In this chapter you will get an overview of what exactly Redash is and what kind of problems Redash tries to solve.

Chapter 2, *Installing Redash*, In this chapter you will be walked through the installation process, there are several options to install Redash, all are covered.

Chapter 3, *Creating and Visualizing your First Query*, chapter for those who want to get right to the point ASAP; a brief overview of everything you need to get started immediately.

Chapter 4, *Connecting to Data Sources*, chapter that introduces the reader to all the DataSources that Redash can connect to, and their options.

Chapter 5, *Writing and Executing Queries*, a chapter that gives a walkthrough of Redash's query editor, that covers everything related to creating, editing and executing queries

Chapter 6, *Creating Visualizations*, chapter that will show all the possible visualization options in Redash, and guidse you on how to use them.

Chapter 7, *Dashboards and Practical Tips*, chapter that covers actions on Dashboards, and some useful general tips for Redash users.

Chapter 8, *Customizing Redash*, Chapter that covers the option to extend and customize Redash for your own specific needs.

To get the most out of this book

1. If you will be the maintainer of a self hosted redash service – you must be proficient with Linux , this will help you to get through Chapter 2, *Installing Redash* chapter.
2. If you will be using Redash to write and visualize queries only – then your minimal requirement will be SQL (no matter which).
3. If you wish to contribute back to redash, or extend its functionality – then Python and some JavaScript knowledge is required.
4. In all of the above cases – you can only benefit if you run the examples presented in the book.
5. from dev side – most of the benefits come from looking at the code!

Download the example code files

You can download the example code files for this book from your account at www.packtpub.com. If you purchased this book elsewhere, you can visit www.packtpub.com/support and register to have the files emailed directly to you.

You can download the code files by following these steps:

1. Log in or register at www.packtpub.com.
2. Select the **SUPPORT** tab.
3. Click on **Code Downloads & Errata**.
4. Enter the name of the book in the **Search** box and follow the onscreen instructions.

Once the file is downloaded, please make sure that you unzip or extract the folder using the latest version of:

- WinRAR/7-Zip for Windows
- Zipeg/iZip/UnRarX for Mac
- 7-Zip/PeaZip for Linux

The code bundle for the book is also hosted on GitHub at `https://github.com/PacktPublishing/Redash-v5-Quick-Start-Guide`. In case there's an update to the code, it will be updated on the existing GitHub repository.

We also have other code bundles from our rich catalog of books and videos available at `https://github.com/PacktPublishing/`. Check them out!

Conventions used

There are a number of text conventions used throughout this book.

`CodeInText`: Indicates code words in text, database table names, folder names, filenames, file extensions, pathnames, dummy URLs, user input, and Twitter handles. Here is an example: "In case you prefer to have more control over the installation, you can choose Docker or manually run the `bootstrap.sh` script"

A block of code is set as follows:

```
root@ip-10-69-10-45:/home/bitnami
root@ip-10-69-10-45:/home/bitnami
telnet 54.156.58.190 5432
Trying 54.156.58.190...
Connected to 54.156.58.190.
Escape character is '^]'.
^]
telnet>
```

Any command-line input or output is written as follows:

```
ps -ef | grep redash
```

Bold: Indicates a new term, an important word, or words that you see onscreen. For example, words in menus or dialog boxes appear in the text like this. Here is an example: "To create a new visualization, press the **+New Visualization** button"

Warnings or important notes appear like this.

 Tips and tricks appear like this.

Get in touch

Feedback from our readers is always welcome.

General feedback: Email `feedback@packtpub.com` and mention the book title in the subject of your message. If you have questions about any aspect of this book, please email us at `questions@packtpub.com`.

Errata: Although we have taken every care to ensure the accuracy of our content, mistakes do happen. If you have found a mistake in this book, we would be grateful if you would report this to us. Please visit `www.packtpub.com/submit-errata`, selecting your book, clicking on the Errata Submission Form link, and entering the details.

Piracy: If you come across any illegal copies of our works in any form on the Internet, we would be grateful if you would provide us with the location address or website name. Please contact us at `copyright@packtpub.com` with a link to the material.

If you are interested in becoming an author: If there is a topic that you have expertise in and you are interested in either writing or contributing to a book, please visit `authors.packtpub.com`.

Reviews

Please leave a review. Once you have read and used this book, why not leave a review on the site that you purchased it from? Potential readers can then see and use your unbiased opinion to make purchase decisions, we at Packt can understand what you think about our products, and our authors can see your feedback on their book. Thank you!

For more information about Packt, please visit `packtpub.com`.

Introducing Redash

Nowadays, every business creates vast amounts of data. Whether it's plain logs, usage statistics, or user data, businesses tend to store it.

But without proper analysis and usage, this data just occupies space (S3s, self-hosted Hadoop clusters, regular RDBMS, and so on) and resources (someone must maintain the servers; otherwise, the data is lost).

The ultimate goal is to try to make the data work for the benefit of the company.

Data analysis rapidly expands beyound the domain of enclosed research departments and penetrates almost every department along the company's verticals.

The trend is that data insights move from *business-supporting* to *business-generating* roles.

In this chapter, we will cover the following topics:

- Data challenges experienced by companies on a daily basis
- Ideal tools to target challenges
- Meeting Redash
- Redash architecture

Data challenges experienced by companies on a daily basis

Let's have a look at an abstract example of a social gaming company and it's use of data:

- CEO/SVPs use generic knowledge of company revenues, pre-defined KPIs (new daily users/daily active users/churn rate)
- The marketing/business development departments use conversion funnels/campaign traction/pre-defined KPIs/growth rate/revenues (usually also sliced by department/game type/geolocation).
- The finance department uses various revenue breakdowns (by department/by external clients, and so on)
- The sales department uses revenues by campaigns breakdown (for better campaign evaluation)
- The product department uses statistics/growth rate/feature popularity/new daily users (to find out whether a specific feature attracts more users/revenue (with at least the same slicing as marketing)
- Customer support/QA/developers deal with bug rates/user reviews/usage statistics
- Data analytics/data scientists require data on usage statistics
- IT/DBAs/operations/infrastructure need information regarding load statistics/uptime/response SLAs/disk usage/CPU/memory (and other various system stats)
- External (contractors/clients/partners) require daily/weekly/monthly reports of various business metrics

As you can see, all the different departments rely on data and have their own specific data needs.

We can also note that if we treat each need as a building block, we can reuse them across departments.

But data is not only about numbers. People like to get a *real feel*, and that's where visualization can come in handy, especially when there is a need to discover trends or spot anomalies. Most of the time, it's much easier to track everything through charts and graphs, even if they represent an abstract trend.

Needless to say, each visualization forms a building block too.

All the preceding points can be joined by a dashboard (or, in most cases, dashboards), where every department has at least one of their own.

Moreover, good visualizations, which are tied together to make an understandable and meaningful user journey through the data (like dashboards), are almost mandatory for data-driven decision making (instead of decision making based on a gut feeling).

This data usage pattern is not unique to social gaming companies. In fact, you can easily define a starter pack of KPIs/metrics that are crucial to track the growth of any company.

An example dashboard

(image source: redash.io)

Suppose we want to provide our product department with a **Redash usage dashboard** (based on real Redash usage data), that consists of several metrics:

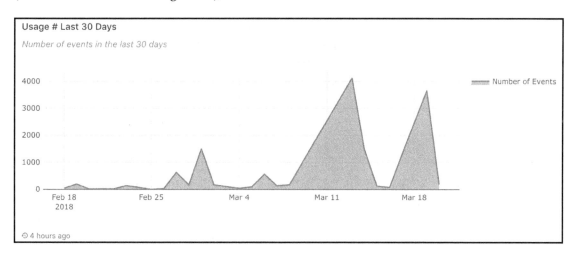

The preceding diagram is a **Usage chart**. Usage can be any form of interaction with Redash. This chart shows us the total amount of interactions with Redash per day over a 30-day period:

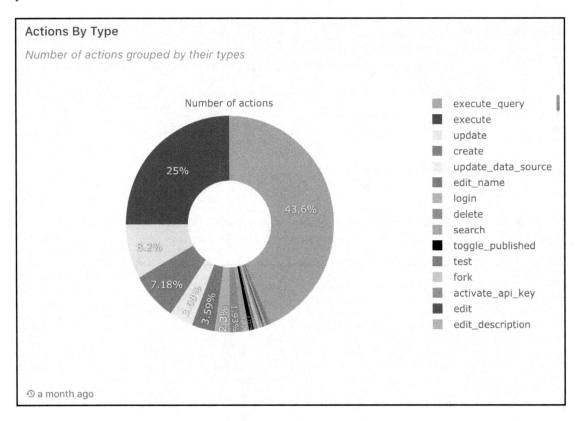

In the preceding chart, we can see that the different events have been broken down into types, which allows us to gain a better understanding of the main use cases of Redash:

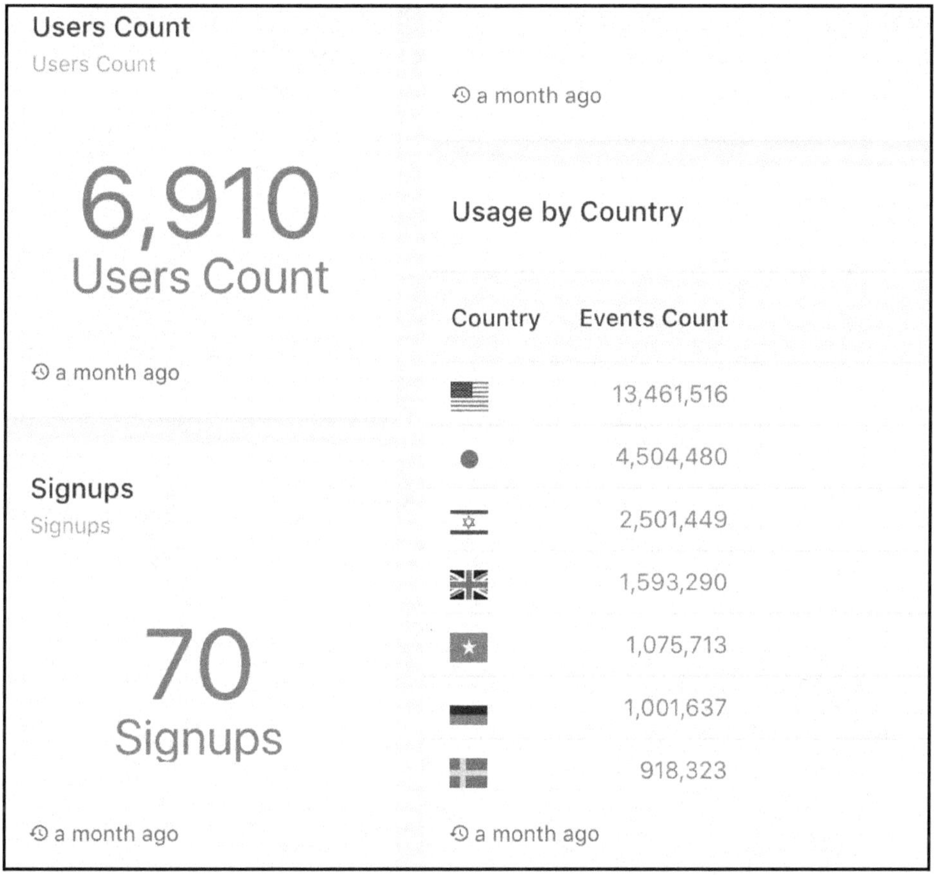

Users Count

Users Count

🕓 a month ago

6,910
Users Count

🕓 a month ago

Signups

Signups

70
Signups

🕓 a month ago

Usage by Country

Country	Events Count
🇺🇸	13,461,516
●	4,504,480
🇮🇱	2,501,449
🇬🇧	1,593,290
★	1,075,713
▬	1,001,637
🇩🇰	918,323

🕓 a month ago

Along with a further breakout of events by Country (gives us a distribution of events in different countries), using IP2Location transformation. In addition to this, there are the new signups and the total user count metrics.

Every single one of these metrics can tell us something valuable, but when combined with a single dashboard (as you can see in the following diagram), a metric can tell us a whole different kind of story (which we will cover in upcoming chapters):

Redash dashboard, themed queries, and visualizations combined

Ideal tools for targeting challenges

Based on the previous example, let's summarize a set of features for an ideal tool that help the company as a whole make the most of its data:

- **Easy to use**: Not everyone in every department is a rocket scientist, so we need the tool to be as simple as possible.

- **Easy to collaborate on**: Since we have already defined the building blocks, it would be great if it can be used and, more importantly, re-used and extended.

  It would be great if *person A* from marketing were to start to create a query and *person B* from sales were able to see it while it's being created, and then comment/modify and create a separate version of it.

  The same goes for query visualizations and dashboards.

- **Shareable**: Preferably online, as there is no need to force anyone to install extra tools on their laptop. It must be flexible in terms of what to share, since we might want to expose it to someone outside the company (contractors/clients/partners).

- **Should support a variety of Data Sources**: Every department has its own Data Sources (the marketing department might have Oracle/MySQL/PostgreSQL, while the IT department might have InfluxDB/ElasticSearch, and so on), and it would be great to have a tool that connects to them all or, even better, a tool that can mix different Data Sources in the same dashboard.

- **Query scheduling/auto-refresh**: We want the dashboards to be up to date every time we look at them.

- **Easily extendable**: The data world changes rapidly; new Data Sources are being created, businesses demand new visualizations, new integrations pop up, and so on. We want to ensure that all of these factors are easily incorporated into our tool.

- **Alerts**: It would be very handy to be able to define critical thresholds for KPIs or metrics and receive an email/slack alert/custom notification if this occurs.

- **API for external integrations**: To fully unleash the power of company data, you can't skip the API part; every developer who has an idea of how to tailor the analytical tool to their own need must be provided with an easy way to do it. The same goes for integrations with external clients/partners who want to access the data programmatically—and what can be easier than the REST API?

- **Fast**: In a rapidly changing world and businesses that grow quickly, *speed is king*. When we say speed, we mean both tool response time and tool-get-the-task-done time. What is the tool worth if it takes half an hour just to create and visualize a single KPI?

Meeting Redash

Back in 2013, a company named EverythingMe was facing all the preceding challenges and yearned for a tool that would have an ideal set of features and fit in with our well-established data-driven culture.

After trying several legacy BI suites, a decision was made to create an easier, more collaborative, and faster tool having `JSFiddle` as inspiration.

These conditions stimulated the creation of Redash to target those requirements.

Redash was created during a hackathon by Arik Fraimovich, who then became the founder and lead developer of Redash.

While initially built to allow rapidly querying and visualizing data from Amazon Redshift (hence the name *Re:Dash = Redshift + Dashboard)*, Redash quickly grew to become the company's main data analysis, visualization, and dashboarding tool, serving all of the departments in the company.

More Data Sources and visualization types were added, people started to contribute to the source code, and eventually Redash was released as an open source tool, and later developed into a separate independent company, with Redash as its main product. Its main goal was to help other companies to become more data-driven with little to no effort, just as we did back in the days at EverythingMe.

What exactly is Redash?

In this paragraph, we will go over the key features of Redash to understand its possibilities and how it can fit into various departments within the company:

- Redash is an open source tool that is used to create, visualize, and share queries and dashboards.
- It works in the browser, so there's no need to install anything on a user's computer: just click the link and log in.
- It's easy to set up and can provide any team member with the immediate power to analyze data.

- Redash is very easy and intuitive to use.

  Even if a team member is not familiar with SQL syntax, they can utilize **query parameters** that they can easily modify to get the desired results, alternatively they can easily **Fork** (**Duplicate**—exactly as you would in GitHub), an existing query/visualization, and modify it according to their needs.

  Both the query parameters and Forking work best as a quick intro into the Redash world.

- Redash allows you to share and embed queries/visualizations/dashboards, which is as easy as sending a URL.
- Redash supports many Data Sources. Whether it's RDBMS, BigData NoSQL, or REST API, you've got them all (a full list and further details are available in `Chapter 4`, *Connecting to Data Sources*). You can even define a query result as a separate datasource and use it later in other queries.
- There are a handful of various visualizations, so everyone in the company will find one that suits their mission best.
- Visualizations can be exported as PNGs, PDFs, and so on.
- Data can be exported as CSV/JSON and Excel.
- Redash includes query scheduling and an auto refresh mechanism.
- Redash provides you with an *alerting* mechanism, where you can define alerts (for example, if the new daily user numbers are below a certain threshold), and then get notifications about it via email/chat/a custom defined webhook.
- Redash provides live auto complete in the query editor and keyboard shortcuts.
- Automatic schema discovery for all Data Sources.
- Results are cached for minimal running times and rapid response. Results from the same query are reused; there is no resource wasting and needless query execution!
- There's SSO, access control, and many other great features for enterprise-friendly workflows, in regard to user management.
- Regarding the API, Redash provides a REST API that allows you to access all of its features programmatically, as well as pass dynamic parameters to queries. This can be used to extend functionality and tailor it to your own department's specific needs.

One example of this concerns data export for external clients, such as sending an automatic daily revenue report. Another great example of API usage is slack chatbot integration, which allows you to easily bring data into team conversations. A proper example of self-service is where any team member can fetch data insights from within a chat window, no coding is required, and there is no need to open tickets to the BI team: just type your request inside the chat and get the results!

- In addition to the API, Redash is open source, which means that you can extend any part you want (this will be covered in `Chapter 8`, *Customizing Redash*).

What if you need a different visualization type? You got it! You need a new datasource? This is a piece of cake. You need a new alert or a new API call? Everything is at your fingertips.

- With over 200 contributors and over 10,000 stars on GitHub, Redash has got a strong and vibrant community, and the project constantly evolves.

In summary, Redash improves—and makes more transparent to peers —a company's decision-making process, based on an easy and speedy creation of deep-dive dashboards over a company's Data Sources.

This speed comes from several aspects:

- There's no entry level barrier, as literally every team member can log in to Redash and start getting insights.
- There are suitable solutions across all the verticals and departments within the company, which eliminates the need to wait for other departments to get the data ready. This is tailored to your needs.
- Self-service is king, as you can fork the queries and modify them as required. You are in full control of your data and visualizations.
- You can query all the possible Data Sources from a single place, and join multiple Data Sources into a single dashboard.

- You can create crucial business alerts to keep you posted as they happen.
- Results are cached for faster retrieving and avoid the generation of useless loads on your Data Sources.
- Instant sharing! Just send the link and you're set.

Redash has two options that you can use: hosted (with monthly subscription plans) or self-hosted Open Source version (free, and you get to maintain it yourself).

The hosted version is suitable for companies who don't want the hassle of hosting and managing the Redash service (and the surrounding components such as Redis/PostgreSQL/Celery) by themselves (usually, this requires at least one or two dedicated employees, and not everyone has them available immediately).

The self-hosted version suits you best when you have the necessary resources (both machine and human) and:

- You want to extend Redash to your own specific needs
- You want to contribute to the open source community
- You want full control over your own data

The hosted and self-hosted versions are identical, and you can always switch back and forth.

It is recommended, however, to try the self-hosted Redash in development mode at the very least, as this way you can gain a better understanding of the internals of the tool that is about to change your company's data culture!

This book will cover only the self-hosted version of Redash (**v5**), all the covered themes are identical to the hosted version of Redash. Most of the themes are fully backwards compatible to versions older than v5, please refer to Redash official website to check the difference.

- Redash's official website can be found at `https://redash.io/`
- Redash's official Git repository can be found at `https://github.com/getredash/redash`
- Redash's knowledge base can be found at `https://redash.io/help/`

Redash architecture

Redash is a single-page web app, with JS frontend and Python backend.

Originally having the frontend written in AngularJS, since V5, it's in transition to React:

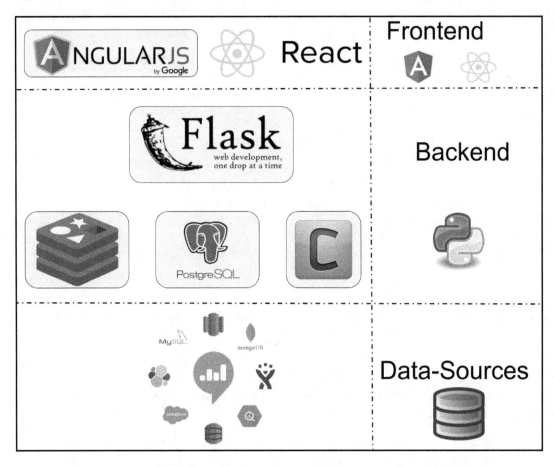

Redash itself is written in Python.

The **UI** (frontend) is **AngularJS,** which is responsible for all the visualizations, dashboards, and the query editor. The regular user interacts with this the most.

The **server** (backend) is a **Flask** App, which uses the **Celery** Distributed Task Queue as its task worker engine (Celery workers are responsible for query execution).

The server handles the actual query execution requests on various Data Sources, such as dashboard refresh requests, both from the frontend and from API calls (for example, slack bots, advanced user's webhooks, and so on).

The **PostgreSQL** database is used to store all the necessary application metadata and configurations (users/groups/datasource definitions/queries/dashboards).

Redis in the memory datastore serves as both the Celery Message Broker (Celery requires a message broker service to send and receive messages).

Summary

In this chapter, we've covered the challenges that every data-driven business should expect to come across, and how Redash comes in handy to target those challenges and help shorten the time between questions and answers by allowing the user to query all of their Data Sources from a single place, without moving the data anywhere.

Redash allows you to combine queries and visualizations from different Data Sources in a single dashboard to provide the business department with the most comprehensive overview possible.

In the sections that followed, we went over the main features of Redash, as well as its architecture in brief. In the next chapter, we will cover the installation options and a step-by-step guide to Redash.

If you're planning to use Redash as a hosted service, or if the installation of the software will be undertaken by another department, you can skip the next chapter.

Installing Redash
2

Once you've decided to go for a self-hosted Redash, it's time to decide which installation you should perform.

 This chapter is intended for people with some knowledge of the Linux operating system. If you choose to install Redash on a machine that already contains production services, take extra care when manually executing operations. You will need root privileges on the machine.

The information you'll find in this chapter has been checked for correctness and is accurate regarding the current version and installation procedure of Redash. For up to date data, please refer to the official Redash website!

- **Setup page**: https://redash.io/help/open-source/setup
- **Dev-guide (always useful)**: https://redash.io/help/open-source/dev-guide/

 Although it is technically possible to run Redash on Windows OS, it is highly recommended that you use a Linux machine, especially for production configuration.

Windows users who want to experiment are encouraged to do so in a VM or a container. Win 10/Windows Server 1709 and later users can take advantage of the Linux subsystem for Windows.

From the Windows official website: The Windows subsystem for Linux lets developers run Linux environments, including most command-line tools, utilities, and applications directly on Windows, unmodified, without the overhead of a virtual machine.

More information on how to install your favorite Linux distribution on Windows can be found here: https://docs.microsoft.com/en-us/windows/wsl/about. After you have installed your Linux distro, continue installing as if you had a native Linux machine.

In this chapter, we will cover the following topics:

- Sizing – choosing the right machine to do the job
- Installation options and installation walkthrough
- Explaining the main setup script
- Troubleshooting
- Configuration and setup
- Permissions in Redash

Sizing – choosing the right machine to do the job

Sizing is based on the number of concurrent users and the number of concurrent queries that you have. For <10 concurrent users and <100 active queries, a tiny machine that has a dual core, 2 GB memory should be enough.

On the other hand, if you have 50-100 concurrent users and 1,000 active queries, you will need at least 16-32 GB RAM and a quad-core CPU.

In addition to the *Redash* app, you will also need Postgres, Redis, and Celery.

- **Redis** - Memory intensive
- **Postgres** - CPU and memory
- **Celery** - CPU and memory (the more workers you have, the more CPU you need. **If workers won't keep up and build up a queue, it starts to consume memory**)

If you're hosted in the cloud, you can always start with a smaller machine and expand if needed. The same goes for deploying Redash inside a VM in your own data center.

As a good starting point, you can use the following instance types on GCE/AWS:

- **On AWS:** t2.medium (2 vCPU, 4 GB RAM)
- **On GCE:** n1-standard-1/ n1-standard-2 (1/2 vCPU and 4/8 GB RAM accordingly)

For more intensive usage:

- **On AWS**: `m4.2xlarge/m5.2xlarge` (both with 8vCPU, 32 GB RAM)
- **On GCE**: `n1-standard-8` (8vCPU, 32 RAM)

Installation options and installation walkthrough

In this section, we will cover the options you have when installing Redash. If your machine resides in the cloud, you will be able to choose an existing image of Redash with all the necessary components already predefined.

In case you prefer to have more control over the installation, you can run the *setup.sh* script or manually run Docker installation.

Installation options

There are various installation options for Redash, and they are as follows:

For the Cloud (AWS/GCE):

- Using a predefined image
- Manually using a Setup script

For your own datacenter (VM or Physical Machine):

- Docker
- Manually using a Setup script

    In all of the aforementioned options, you can provide your own Postgres/Redis, in case you already have them installed.

As we already seen in the Redash architecture chart from the previous chapter, Redash needs Postgres (version 9.3 or newer) and Redis (version 2.8 or newer) to operate.

Both Postgres and Redis **can** be installed separately (if you already have them installed, then you can configure Redash to use them using environment variables).

Redash releases are located here: `https://github.com/getredash/redash/releases`.

AWS-predefined image

This is a very easy type of installation, since everything is packed into a convenient image. To pick a specific image, you can either find it here: `https://redash.io/help/open-source/setup#aws`, or pick up the suitable **AMI (Amazon Machine Image)** and look up the image manually, as shown in the following screenshot:

The screenshot actions are explained as follows:

1. Select the **AMI** section in EC2 console
2. Select **Public Images** from the dropdown list
3. Type **redash** to search for Redash related images
4. Select the desired Redash image (the selected image is v5 official AMI by Redash) marked with **4***, which is the alternative Redash image, by Bitnami

Bitnami is a company (not related to Redash) that specifies on packaging, deploying, and maintaining web applications.

Note - to use the AWS Marketplace **Bitnami** images, you first need to accept the terms and conditions and subscribe.

After you have found the AMI of your choice, you can proceed to machine selection and launch it. When launching the instance, you must configure a security group (in AWS - A *security group* acts as a virtual firewall for the machine you launched, to control inbound and outbound traffic.).

You will need the following ports for inbound traffic (it's best to consult your networking specialist on best practices for firewall rules):

- port 22 (SSH).
- port 80 (HTTP).
- port 443 (HTTPS).

Note that Redash AMIs are based on Ubuntu, so the user is **ubuntu** when connecting to the instance via SSH.

In Bitnami images, the user is **bitnami**.

Launching an instance using Redash AMI

After selecting the Redash AMI, you can launch an instance from that image.

After the machine is up and running, find the public IP or the DNS name of the machine in order to log in to the Redash.

After obtaining the IP/DNS, simply enter either of them in your browser, and you should be viewing the Redash Initial Setup page (page seen when logging in to Redash for the very first time):

If for any reason you can't see that page (or you see errors) it means that the installation didn't finish successfully, and you need to refer to server logs for further details.

To obtain the server logs, do the following:

Right click on the instance in the AWS EC2 console, and go to **Instance Settings | Get System Log**:

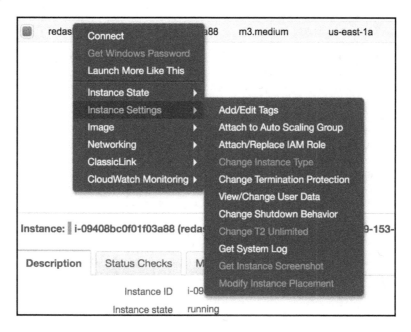

The log will open in a pop-up window.

Launching an instance using Bitnami Redash AMI

In case you decided to use Bitnami AMI, the steps are mostly identical to Redash's official AMI.

After the instance is ready, you need to find out its public **IP / DNS** and open the **System Log** of the instance to get the user/pass so that you can log in to Redash.

Here is a relevant part from the system log of the instance we started in the previous example:

```
[    44.581715] bitnami[314]: large
[    45.784949] ip_tables: (C) 2000-2006 Netfilter Core Team
[    46.575518] bitnami[314]:
###################################################################
[    46.592191] bitnami[314]: #
#
[    46.609797] bitnami[314]: #         Setting Bitnami application password
to 'k4gs94SvhRBW'          #
[    46.624549] bitnami[314]: #         (the default application username is
'user@example.com')          #
[    46.640013] bitnami[314]: #
#
[    46.655361] bitnami[314]:
###################################################################
[[32m  OK [0m] Started LSB: Cloud init local.
         Starting LSB: Cloud init...
[[32m  OK [0m] Started LSB: Cloud init.
         Starting LSB: Cloud init modules --mode config...
         Starting OpenBSD Secure Shell server...
```

From the preceding log, we can find the **user/pass** so that we can log in to Redash.

In case of Bitnami image, the first phase setup (that is, the creation of the Redash Admin user) is done by Bitnami, and you are redirected to the Login page itself.

Now, we simply point the browser to the public **IP / DNS** of the instance.

If everything goes as expected, we should see the login page of Redash, as follows:

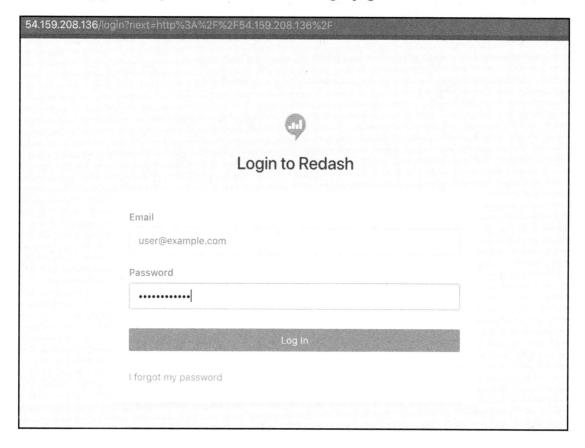

Welcome to Redash setup page

After creating the Admin user (in case of Redash AMI) or logging in using the credentials found in the system log (in case of Bitnami AMI), we should see the following screen, where the user will be guided through a short quickstart setup:

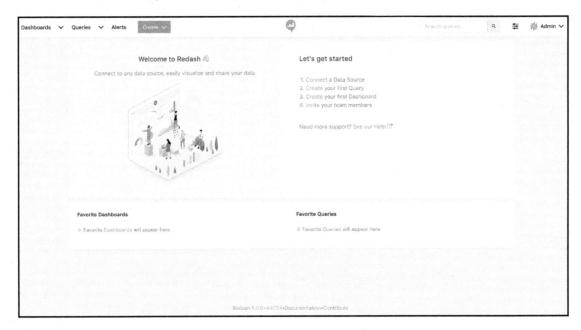

Before we can declare the installation as complete, let's SSH to the machine and check what processes are running there. In our example, the user is **bitnami**.

First, we SSH into the machine using the following code:

```
ssh -i $PATH_TO_YOUR_PEM_KEY bitnami@$PUBLIC_IP_OF_THE_MACHINE
```

When inside the machine, run the following code:

```
ps -ef | grep redash
```

We should get something similar to the following output:

redash_gunicorn - redash web app (we can see the parent process with pid 1912, and 4 child processes: 2052, 2053, 2054, 2055):

```
redash 1912 1 0 May13 ? 00:02:07
/opt/bitnami/apps/redash/htdocs/venv/bin/python
/opt/bitnami/apps/redash/htdocs/venv/bin/gunicorn -b 127.0.0.1:5000 --pid
```

```
/opt/bitnami/apps/redash/logs/redash_gunicorn.pid --log-file
/opt/bitnami/apps/redash/logs/redash_gunicorn.log --name redash -w 4 --max-
requests 1000 redash.wsgi:app

redash 2052 1912 0 May13 ? 00:00:18
/opt/bitnami/apps/redash/htdocs/venv/bin/python
/opt/bitnami/apps/redash/htdocs/venv/bin/gunicorn -b 127.0.0.1:5000 --pid
/opt/bitnami/apps/redash/logs/redash_gunicorn.pid --log-efile
/opt/bitnami/apps/redash/logs/redash_gunicorn.log --name redash -w 4 --max-
requests 1000 redash.wsgi:app

 redash 2053 1912 0 May13 ? 00:00:19
/opt/bitnami/apps/redash/htdocs/venv/bin/python
/opt/bitnami/apps/redash/htdocs/venv/bin/gunicorn -b 127.0.0.1:5000 --pid
/opt/bitnami/apps/redash/logs/redash_gunicorn.pid --log-file
/opt/bitnami/apps/redash/logs/redash_gunicorn.log --name redash -w 4 --max-
requests 1000 redash.wsgi:app

redash 2054 1912 0 May13 ? 00:00:19
/opt/bitnami/apps/redash/htdocs/venv/bin/python
/opt/bitnami/apps/redash/htdocs/venv/bin/gunicorn -b 127.0.0.1:5000 --pid
/opt/bitnami/apps/redash/logs/redash_gunicorn.pid --log-file
/opt/bitnami/apps/redash/logs/redash_gunicorn.log --name redash -w 4 --max-
requests 1000 redash.wsgi:app

redash 2055 1912 0 May13 ? 00:00:20
/opt/bitnami/apps/redash/htdocs/venv/bin/python
/opt/bitnami/apps/redash/htdocs/venv/bin/gunicorn -b 127.0.0.1:5000 --pid
/opt/bitnami/apps/redash/logs/redash_gunicorn.pid --log-file
/opt/bitnami/apps/redash/logs/redash_gunicorn.log --name redash -w 4 --max-
requests 1000 redash.wsgi:app
```

The job of Celery worker processes (which has a parent with a pid of 1934 and 3 child processes) is to run the ad-hoc queries as well as other tasks (for example, sending an email):

```
 redash 1934 1 0 May13 ? 00:37:54
/opt/bitnami/apps/redash/htdocs/venv/bin/python
/opt/bitnami/apps/redash/htdocs/venv/bin/celery worker --pidfile
/opt/bitnami/apps/redash/logs/redash_celery_worker.pid --app=redash.worker
--beat -c2 -Qqueries,celery --maxtasksperchild=10 -Ofair
redash 2058 1934 0 May13 ? 00:01:27
/opt/bitnami/apps/redash/htdocs/venv/bin/python
/opt/bitnami/apps/redash/htdocs/venv/bin/celery worker --pidfile
/opt/bitnami/apps/redash/logs/redash_celery_worker.pid --app=redash.worker
--beat -c2 -Qqueries,celery --maxtasksperchild=10 -Ofair
 redash 28495 1934 0 09:02 ? 00:00:01
/opt/bitnami/apps/redash/htdocs/venv/bin/python
```

```
/opt/bitnami/apps/redash/htdocs/venv/bin/celery worker --pidfile
/opt/bitnami/apps/redash/logs/redash_celery_worker.pid --app=redash.worker
--beat -c2 -Qqueries,celery --maxtasksperchild=10 -Ofair
 redash 28502 1934 0 09:04 ? 00:00:01
/opt/bitnami/apps/redash/htdocs/venv/bin/python
/opt/bitnami/apps/redash/htdocs/venv/bin/celery worker --pidfile
/opt/bitnami/apps/redash/logs/redash_celery_worker.pid --app=redash.worker
--beat -c2 -Qqueries,celery --maxtasksperchild=10 -Ofair
```

Celery's scheduled queries queue worker processes (which has a parent with a pid of 1955 and 2 children), and their task is to process the scheduled queries:

```
 redash 1955 1 0 May13 ? 00:18:51
/opt/bitnami/apps/redash/htdocs/venv/bin/python
/opt/bitnami/apps/redash/htdocs/venv/bin/celery worker --pidfile
/opt/bitnami/apps/redash/logs/redash_celery_scheduled.pid --
app=redash.worker -c2 -Qscheduled_queries --maxtasksperchild=10 -Ofair

 redash 2047 1955 0 May13 ? 00:00:01
/opt/bitnami/apps/redash/htdocs/venv/bin/python
/opt/bitnami/apps/redash/htdocs/venv/bin/celery worker --pidfile
/opt/bitnami/apps/redash/logs/redash_celery_scheduled.pid --
app=redash.worker -c2 -Qscheduled_queries --maxtasksperchild=10 -Ofair

 redash 2061 1955 0 May13 ? 00:00:01
/opt/bitnami/apps/redash/htdocs/venv/bin/python
/opt/bitnami/apps/redash/htdocs/venv/bin/celery worker --pidfile
/opt/bitnami/apps/redash/logs/redash_celery_scheduled.pid --
app=redash.worker -c2 -Qscheduled_queries --maxtasksperchild=10 -Ofair
```

PostgreSQL database processes:

```
 postgres 2138 842 0 May13 ? 00:00:00 postgres: bn_redash bitnami_redash
127.0.0.1(58991) idle
 postgres 2142 842 0 May13 ? 00:00:00 postgres: bn_redash bitnami_redash
127.0.0.1(59000) idle
 postgres 2161 842 0 May13 ? 00:00:00 postgres: bn_redash bitnami_redash
127.0.0.1(59007) idle
 postgres 2440 842 0 May13 ? 00:00:00 postgres: bn_redash bitnami_redash
127.0.0.1(59070) idle
 postgres 28499 842 0 09:03 ? 00:00:00 postgres: bn_redash bitnami_redash
127.0.0.1(43470) idle
 postgres 28507 842 0 09:05 ? 00:00:00 postgres: bn_redash bitnami_redash
127.0.0.1(43473) idle
```

From the preceding code, we can see the following:

- Postgres DB process (and its workers)
- Redis
- Celery workers
- Gunicorn: The WSGI HTTP Server (that actually serves the *Redash* app)

Now, we can consider the installation as complete.

GCE-Predefined image

This installation process is very similar to AWS. GCE also benefits from both Redash official image, as well as Bitnami image.

In order to use the official Redash image - you have to add it to your account first.

Use the following command:

```
gcloud compute images create "redash-5-0-0" --source-uri gs://redash-images/redash.5.0.0.b4754.tar.gz
```

The output of running the preceding command should be similar to the following:

```
macbook-alexleb:Redash-Quick-Start-Guide ext_alexanderl$ gcloud compute images create "redash-5-0-0" --source-uri gs://redash-images/redash.5.0.0.b4754.tar.gz

Created [https://www.googleapis.com/compute/v1/projects/re3dashtest/global/images/redash-5-0-0].
NAME          PROJECT       FAMILY  DEPRECATED  STATUS
redash-5-0-0  re3dashtest                       READY
```

After validating that the image is created in your account, you can proceed to selecting this image, and creating an instance.

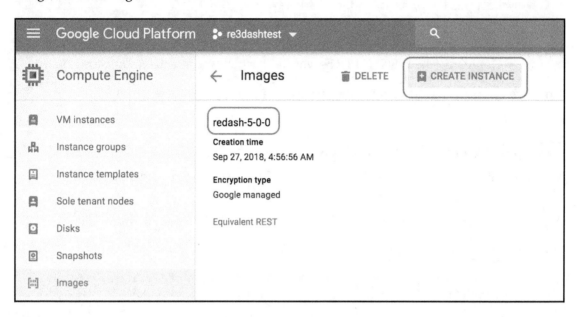

In case you wish to use Bitnami image, it already comes packaged as Virtual Machine - simply search it in the GCE search box, and select the "Redash certified by Bitnami" option.

The estimated cost is not the cost of the **Bitnami** image, but the cost of the machine, as shown in the following screenshot:

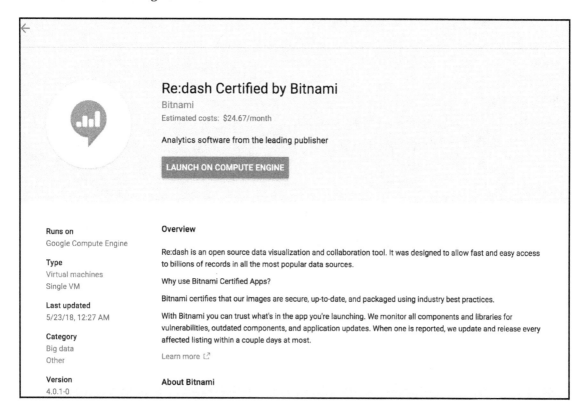

After deciding to Launch the VM, go ahead and choose the machine type:

After your specified machine is up and running, you can find its IP, username, and password in the properties page:

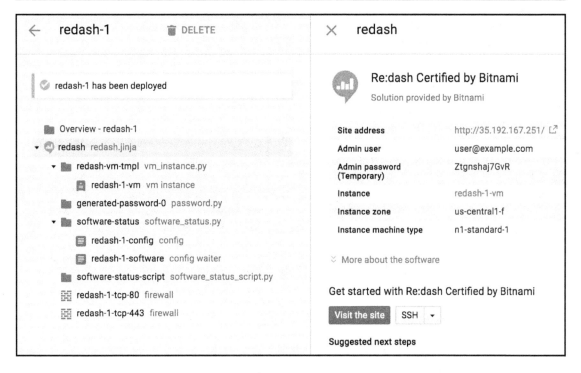

After you have found the IP, username, and password, you can log in and validate that the installation was successful.

Docker-based installation

You can install Docker from the following link: `https://docs.docker.com/install/`.

After installing Docker we can proceed to Redash installation

1. Clone the Redash repository (or download a `.zip` release).
2. Make sure you have a Docker machine up and running.
3. Make sure your current working directory is the root of this GitHub repository.
4. Use the `docker-compose.production.yml` configuration file and modify the configuration values as needed. For example, you may want to change these:
   - The Postgres volume location
   - The value of `REDASH_COOKIE_SECRET` (especially if this instance is not just for testing purposes)

2. Run `docker-compose -f docker-compose.production.yml run --rm server create_db` to set up the database.
3. Run `docker-compose -f docker-compose.production.yml up`.
4. Redash should be available on port 80 of the host machine.

`docker-compose.yml` overview:

The following is an example configuration for Docker Compose. It is recommended that you update the cookie secret (used as the Redash browser cookie) and Postgres database password.
In order to persist Postgres data, assign it a volume host location. You can also split the worker service to ad hoc workers and scheduled queries workers (ad hoc workers will perform the execution of nonscheduled queries, as well as other tasks like sending emails and so on).

Scheduled services, as their name suggests, will perform the periodic execution of all scheduled queries.

In the file we can see the definition of the following:

- redash server - the main Redash server
- celery scheduler
- celery worker for scheduled queries
- celery worker for adhoc queries
- redis server
- postgres server - the Redash's operational db
- nginx - serves as proxy for the Redash server

```yaml
version: '2'
x-redash-service: &redash-service
  image: redash/redash:5.0.0.b4754
  depends_on:
    - postgres
    - redis
  env_file: /opt/redash/env
  restart: always
services:
  server:
    <<: *redash-service
    command: server
    ports:
      - "5000:5000"
    environment:
```

```
    REDASH_WEB_WORKERS: 4
scheduler:
  <<: *redash-service
  command: scheduler
  environment:
    QUEUES: "celery"
    WORKERS_COUNT: 1
scheduled_worker:
  <<: *redash-service
  command: worker
  environment:
    QUEUES: "scheduled_queries"
    WORKERS_COUNT: 1
adhoc_worker:
  <<: *redash-service
  command: worker
  environment:
    QUEUES: "queries"
    WORKERS_COUNT: 2
redis:
  image: redis:3.0-alpine
  restart: always
postgres:
  image: postgres:9.5.6-alpine
  env_file: /opt/redash/env
  volumes:
    - /opt/redash/postgres-data:/var/lib/postgresql/data
  restart: always
nginx:
  image: redash/nginx:latest
  ports:
    - "80:80"
  depends_on:
    - server
  links:
    - server:redash
  restart: always
```

Provisioning script installation

- Locate the setup.sh script (either in .zip or source).
- You have to be the root user in order to run it.
- This script was only tested on Ubuntu 18.04.

- It's designed to run on a clean machine. If you're running this script on a machine that is used for other purposes, you might want to tweak it to your needs.
- Run the `setup.sh` script, it should install Docker based Redash.

Explaining the setup.sh script

The **setup.sh** script is the core of all the cloud based installation options. Regarding an image-based installation, you don't have to dive into the details of this script, but if you want to install Redash manually (or are just curious about the internals), it's better to take a quick look at it.

In case you intend to use the `setup.sh` script for production environment:

For **small scale deployments** you can use it **as is**.

But for large scale deployments where Redash is mission critical, and needs to be Highly Available, it's recommend that you set up a separate server for PostgreSQL and Redis, as well as set up at least 2 servers for Redash for redundancy.

The number of celery workers can be modified based on your usage patterns.

Let's break the script into parts while going over it.

At first, we set Redash base installation path, and start defining helper functions.

The following is the definition of helper function, which installs the docker compose as well as surrounding components:

```bash
#!/usr/bin/env bash
# This script setups dockerized Redash on Ubuntu 18.04.
set -eu

REDASH_BASE_PATH=/opt/redash

install_docker(){
    # Install Docker
    sudo apt-get update
    sudo apt-get -yy install apt-transport-https ca-certificates curl
software-properties-common wget pwgen
    curl -fsSL https://download.docker.com/linux/ubuntu/gpg | sudo apt-key
```

```
add -
    sudo add-apt-repository "deb [arch=amd64]
https://download.docker.com/linux/ubuntu $(lsb_release -cs) stable"
    sudo apt-get update && sudo apt-get -y install docker-ce

    # Install Docker Compose
    sudo curl -L
https://github.com/docker/compose/releases/download/1.22.0/docker-compose-$
(uname -s)-$(uname -m) -o /usr/local/bin/docker-compose
    sudo chmod +x /usr/local/bin/docker-compose

    # Allow current user to run Docker commands
    sudo usermod -aG docker $USER
    newgrp docker
}
```

The following is a helper function that creates the directories for Redash installation:

```
create_directories() {
    if [[ ! -e $REDASH_BASE_PATH ]]; then
        sudo mkdir -p $REDASH_BASE_PATH
        sudo chown $USER:$USER $REDASH_BASE_PATH
    fi

    if [[ ! -e $REDASH_BASE_PATH/postgres-data ]]; then
        mkdir $REDASH_BASE_PATH/postgres-data
    fi
}
```

The following is a helper function that creates and persists Environment Variables used in Redash:

```
create_config() {
    if [[ -e $REDASH_BASE_PATH/env ]]; then
        rm $REDASH_BASE_PATH/env
        touch $REDASH_BASE_PATH/env
    fi

    COOKIE_SECRET=$(pwgen -1s 32)
    POSTGRES_PASSWORD=$(pwgen -1s 32)
REDASH_DATABASE_URL="postgresql://postgres:${POSTGRES_PASSWORD}@postgres/po
stgres"

    echo "PYTHONUNBUFFERED=0" >> $REDASH_BASE_PATH/env
    echo "REDASH_LOG_LEVEL=INFO" >> $REDASH_BASE_PATH/env
    echo "REDASH_REDIS_URL=redis://redis:6379/0" >> $REDASH_BASE_PATH/env
    echo "POSTGRES_PASSWORD=$POSTGRES_PASSWORD" >> $REDASH_BASE_PATH/env
    echo "REDASH_COOKIE_SECRET=$COOKIE_SECRET" >> $REDASH_BASE_PATH/env
```

```
        echo "REDASH_DATABASE_URL=$REDASH_DATABASE_URL" >>
$REDASH_BASE_PATH/env
    }
```

The following helper function fetches the latest docker image, as well as docker-compose file, and runs it:

```
setup_compose() {
    REQUESTED_CHANNEL=stable
    LATEST_VERSION=`curl -s
"https://version.redash.io/api/releases?channel=$REQUESTED_CHANNEL" |
json_pp | grep "docker_image" | head -n 1 | awk 'BEGIN{FS=":"}{print $3}'
| awk 'BEGIN{FS="\""}{print $1}'`

    cd $REDASH_BASE_PATH
    REDASH_BRANCH="${REDASH_BRANCH:-master}" # Default branch/version to
master if not specified in REDASH_BRANCH env var
    wget
https://raw.githubusercontent.com/getredash/redash/${REDASH_BRANCH}/setup/d
ocker-compose.yml
    sed -ri "s/image: redash\/redash:([A-Za-z0-9.-]*)/image:
redash\/redash:$LATEST_VERSION/" docker-compose.yml
    echo "export COMPOSE_PROJECT_NAME=redash" >> ~/.profile
    echo "export COMPOSE_FILE=/opt/redash/docker-compose.yml" >> ~/.profile
    source ~/.profile
    docker-compose run --rm server create_db
    docker-compose up -d
}
```

The following code invokes all the previously defined functions (the order here is important):

```
install_docker
create_directories
create_config
setup_compose
```

Troubleshooting

The main thing to bear in mind here is that setup.sh (core of all the installation processes) is not idempotent.

This means that if somehow the script failed in the middle of running, you can't simply run it again.

In case something went wrong with the installation, follow these instructions:

1. Try to check the output of the `setup.sh` script and figure out what the reason for its failure could be. Possible reasons include permissions/missing packages.
2. It's always better to reinstall rather than try and run the script from where it stopped.
3. Review the section which explains `setup.sh`, in combination with the logs. This might give you the answer.
4. If using AWS/GCE, verify that ports `22`, `80`, and `443` are reachable (sometimes, even if not in the cloud, corporate users have strict firewall rules, so you might have to check it even if not on AWS/GCE).

Configuration and setup

In order to experience Redash to its fullest, after installing it, you need to run some configurations, for example, for users and emails.

Email configuration

Redash uses email as part of user management (password reset and so on) and as a destination for alerts to be received at.

After your first setup, when you log in to Redash, you will see the following notification telling you that your email has not yet been configured, which means that you can't enjoy all the features of Redash:

The email configuration resides inside an `env` file.

We can use the `find` or `locate` Linux command to find where exactly the `env` file resides on our machine.

By default (in case you used setup.sh based installation), it's located at `/opt/redash/env`.

In the bitnami installation for example, the file is located at `/opt/bitnami/apps/redash/htdocs/env`) (in other installations, you can always search for the `env` file if you're not sure where is it located).

Inside the `env` file, lots of values have defaults (localhost, for example), so in case you have postfix (or some other email server) running on the same host as Redash, you can leave the configuration settings as is. Otherwise, you will have to alter the following settings (inside the `env` file):

```
# Note that not all values are required, as they have default values
export REDASH_MAIL_SERVER="" # default: localhost
export REDASH_MAIL_PORT="" # default: 25
export REDASH_MAIL_USE_TLS="" # default: false
export REDASH_MAIL_USE_SSL="" # default: false
export REDASH_MAIL_USERNAME="" # default: None
export REDASH_MAIL_PASSWORD="" # default: None
export REDASH_MAIL_DEFAULT_SENDER="" # Email address to send from
export REDASH_HOST="" # base address of your Redash instance, for example:
"https://demo.redash.io"
```

Once you have updated the configuration, restart all services with `docker-compose up -d`. If you are using a bitnami image and you want to restart all the services, you will have to use the following code:

```
sudo /opt/bitnami/ctlscript.sh restart
```

The output should show you what services were restarted and whether they went up normally.

In the following command output (since we executed a *restart*), we can see the shutdown of all the services (with the order being preserved), and the startup right after (in reverse order):

```
Syntax OK
/opt/bitnami/apache2/scripts/ctl.sh : httpd stopped
/opt/bitnami/apps/redash/scripts/ctl_redash_gunicorn.sh : gunicorn stopped
/opt/bitnami/apps/redash/scripts/ctl_redash_celery_worker.sh : redash-
celery stopped
/opt/bitnami/apps/redash/scripts/ctl_redash_celery_scheduled.sh :
```

```
redash_celery_scheduled stopped
 /opt/bitnami/redis/scripts/ctl.sh : redis stopped
 waiting for server to shut down.... done
 server stopped
 /opt/bitnami/postgresql/scripts/ctl.sh : postgresql stopped
 waiting for server to start.... done
 server started
 /opt/bitnami/postgresql/scripts/ctl.sh : postgresql started at port 5432
 /opt/bitnami/redis/scripts/ctl.sh : redis started at port 6379
 /opt/bitnami/apps/redash/scripts/ctl_redash_gunicorn.sh : gunicorn started
 /opt/bitnami/apps/redash/scripts/ctl_redash_celery_worker.sh :
redash_celery_worker started
 /opt/bitnami/apps/redash/scripts/ctl_redash_celery_scheduled.sh :
redash_celery_scheduled started
 Syntax OK
 /opt/bitnami/apache2/scripts/ctl.sh : httpd started at port 80

root@ip-10-69-10-45:/home/bitnami#
```

 Not all of the values are required, as most of them have defaults.

 It is recommended that you use email services that can ensure delivery (for production or mission critical tasks), for example, SES, Mailgun, or Google email services.

To test the email configuration setting, you can run the following from your command line (from /opt/redash/):

```
docker-compose run --rm server manage send_test_mail
```

For example, for bitnami installation, the command will be as follows:

```
/opt/bitnami/apps/redash/htdocs# ./bin/run
/opt/bitnami/apps/redash/htdocs/manage.py send_test_email
```

When you run **Send Email** from the UI, it will look like this (**1 – press the send email button, 2 – you should see a notification that the email was sent**):

If you didn't get an email after this, the wisest place to look for clues is the logs:

```
$REDASH_INSTALLATION_PATH/logs/redash_celery_worker.log
```

 Once again, note that in different installations, the log location might differ. However, the log name stays the same, so you can always search for it.

Here, we can see a real example of an unauthorized email sending attempt, with incorrect credentials:

```
[2018-06-24 21:46:09,096][PID:2114][WARNING][MainProcess]
celery@ip-10-69-10-45 ready.
 [2018-06-24 21:46:10,690][PID:2147][ERROR][Worker-2]
task_name=redash.tasks.send_mail taks_id=adc52790-4e09-4ced-
ab6e-375689db3676 Failed sending message: Reset your password
 Traceback (most recent call last):
 File "/opt/bitnami/apps/redash/htdocs/redash/tasks/general.py", line 57,
in send_mail
 mail.send(message)
```

```
 File "/opt/bitnami/apps/redash/htdocs/venv/lib/python2.7/site-
packages/flask_mail.py", line 492, in send
  message.send(connection)
 File "/opt/bitnami/apps/redash/htdocs/venv/lib/python2.7/site-
packages/flask_mail.py", line 427, in send
  connection.send(self)
 File "/opt/bitnami/apps/redash/htdocs/venv/lib/python2.7/site-
packages/flask_mail.py", line 192, in send
  message.rcpt_options)
 File "/opt/bitnami/python/lib/python2.7/smtplib.py", line 737, in sendmail
  raise SMTPSenderRefused(code, resp, from_addr)
  SMTPSenderRefused: (530, '5.5.1 Authentication Required. Learn more
at\n5.5.1 https://support.google.com/mail/?p=WantAuthError m14-
v6sbj2132487123dslkj.88 - gsmtp', u'neo.andersson@gmail.com')
```

Using Google OAuth to log in to Redash

If you want to use Google OAuth to authenticate users, you need to create a Google
Developers project (see the instructions (`https://redash.io/help/open-source/admin-guide/google-developer-account-setup`) for this and then add the following
configuration in the `env` file):

```
export REDASH_GOOGLE_CLIENT_ID=""
export REDASH_GOOGLE_CLIENT_SECRET=""
```

Once enabled, Redash will use Google OAuth to authenticate *existing* user accounts. In
order to enable automatic user creation according to a specific domain name, you can add
this domain in the setting page.

If you're passing multiple domains, separate them with commas:

1. Restart the web server to apply the configuration changes: `docker-compose up -d`.

2. Once you have Google OAuth enabled, you can log in using your Google Apps
   account. If you want to grant admin permissions to some users, you can do this
   by adding them to the admin group (from the **/groups** page).

3. If you don't use Google OAuth or just need username/password logins, you can
   create additional users by opening the **/users/new** page.

Redash environment settings

Many aspects of the functionality of Redash can be changes with settings. Settings are read by the `redash.settings` module, from environment variables, which (for **setup.sh** based installs) can be set in the `/opt/redash/env` file.

The following table shows a full list of settings and what they control:

Name	Comments	Default Value
REDASH_REDIS_URL	The URL of the Redis KV Store	redis://localhost:6379/0
REDASH_PROXIES_COUNT		1
REDASH_DATABASE_URL	Redash's applicative DB URL	postgresql://postgres
REDASH_CELERY_BROKER		REDIS_URL
REDASH_CELERY_BACKEND		CELERY_BROKER
REDASH_CELERY_TASK_RESULT_EXPIRES	How many seconds to keep Celery task results in the cache (in seconds)	3600 * 4
REDASH_QUERY_RESULTS_CLEANUP_ENABLED		true
REDASH_QUERY_RESULTS_CLEANUP_COUNT		100
REDASH_QUERY_RESULTS_CLEANUP_MAX_AGE		7
REDASH_SCHEMAS_REFRESH_SCHEDULE	How often to refresh the Data Source schemas (in minutes)	30
REDASH_AUTH_TYPE		api_key
REDASH_ENFORCE_HTTPS		false
REDASH_INVITATION_TOKEN_MAX_AGE		60 * 60 * 24 * 7
REDASH_MULTI_ORG		false
REDASH_GOOGLE_CLIENT_ID		
REDASH_GOOGLE_CLIENT_SECRET		
REDASH_REMOTE_USER_LOGIN_ENABLED		false
REDASH_REMOTE_USER_HEADER		X-Forwarded-Remote-User
REDASH_STATIC_ASSETS_PATH		"../client/dist/"
REDASH_JOB_EXPIRY_TIME		3600 * 12
REDASH_COOKIE_SECRET		c292a0a3aa32397cdb050e233733900f

Name	Comments	Default Value
REDASH_LOG_LEVEL		INFO
REDASH_HOST		
REDASH_ALERTS_DEFAULT_MAIL_SUBJECT_TEMPLATE		({state}) {alert_name}
REDASH_THROTTLE_LOGIN_PATTERN		50/hour
REDASH_LIMITER_STORAGE		REDIS_URL
REDASH_ENABLED_QUERY_RUNNERS		",".join(default_query_runners)
REDASH_ADDITIONAL_QUERY_RUNNERS		
REDASH_DISABLED_QUERY_RUNNERS		
REDASH_ADHOC_QUERY_TIME_LIMIT		None
REDASH_ENABLED_DESTINATIONS		",".join(default_destinations)
REDASH_ADDITIONAL_DESTINATIONS		
REDASH_EVENT_REPORTING_WEBHOOKS		
REDASH_SENTRY_DSN		
REDASH_ALLOW_SCRIPTS_IN_USER_INPUT	Disables sanitization of text input, allowing full HTML	false
REDASH_DASHBOARD_REFRESH_INTERVALS		60,300,600,1800,3600,43200,86400
REDASH_QUERY_REFRESH_INTERVALS		60, 300, 600, 900, 1800, 3600, 7200, 10800, 14400, 18000, 21600, 25200, 28800, 32400, 36000, 39600, 43200, 86400, 604800, 1209600, 2592000
REDASH_DATE_FORMAT		DD/MM/YY
REDASH_FEATURE_SHOW_QUERY_RESULTS_COUNT	Disables/enables showing the count of query results in a status	true
REDASH_VERSION_CHECK		true
REDASH_FEATURE_DISABLE_REFRESH_QUERIES	Disables the scheduled query execution	false
REDASH_FEATURE_SHOW_PERMISSIONS_CONTROL		false
REDASH_FEATURE_ALLOW_CUSTOM_JS_VISUALIZATIONS		false
REDASH_FEATURE_DUMB_RECENTS		false
REDASH_FEATURE_AUTO_PUBLISH_NAMED_QUERIES		true
REDASH_BIGQUERY_HTTP_TIMEOUT		600

Name	Comments	Default Value
REDASH_SCHEMA_RUN_TABLE_SIZE_CALCULATIONS		false
REDASH_ALLOW_PARAMETERS_IN_EMBEDS		false

The following are the `StatsD` settings (daemon for stats aggregation):

Name	Comments	Default values
REDASH_STATSD_HOST		127.0.0.1
REDASH_STATSD_PORT		8125
REDASH_STATSD_PREFIX		redash
REDASH_STATSD_USE_TAGS	Whether to use tags in StatsD metrics (InfluxDB's format)	false

The following are the **CORS** (**Cros Origin Resource Sharing**) settings:

Name	Comments	Default values
REDASH_CORS_ACCESS_CONTROL_ALLOW_ORIGIN		
REDASH_CORS_ACCESS_CONTROL_ALLOW_CREDENTIALS		false
REDASH_CORS_ACCESS_CONTROL_REQUEST_METHOD		GET, POST, PUT
REDASH_CORS_ACCESS_CONTROL_ALLOW_HEADERS		Content-Type

The following are the `LDAP` settings:

Name	Comments	Default values
REDASH_LDAP_LOGIN_ENABLED		false
REDASH_LDAP_URL		None
REDASH_LDAP_BIND_DN		None
REDASH_LDAP_BIND_DN_PASSWORD		

REDASH_LDAP_DISPLAY_NAME_KEY		displayName
REDASH_LDAP_EMAIL_KEY		mail
REDASH_LDAP_CUSTOM_USERNAME_PROMPT		LDAP/AD/SSO username:
REDASH_LDAP_SEARCH_TEMPLATE		(cn=%(username)s)
REDASH_LDAP_SEARCH_DN		REDASH_SEARCH_DN

The following are the mail server settings:

Name	Comments	Default values
REDASH_MAIL_SERVER		localhost
REDASH_MAIL_PORT		25
REDASH_MAIL_USE_TLS		false
REDASH_MAIL_USE_SSL		false
REDASH_MAIL_USERNAME		None
REDASH_MAIL_PASSWORD		None
REDASH_MAIL_DEFAULT_SENDER		None
REDASH_MAIL_MAX_EMAILS		None
REDASH_MAIL_ASCII_ATTACHMENTS		false

HTTPS (SSL) Setup

In case you wish to set up HTTPS access to Redash, and your Redash installation is **setup.sh** based, you can simply update the nginx config file located at `/etc/nginx/sites-available/redash` with SSL configuration.

You will also have to upload the certificate to the server, and set the paths correctly in the new config.

In case of installation without Nginx as proxy - you have to set up something similar to nginx / httpd by yourself, and add the necessary ssl config.

 For Cloud based installations, make sure port 443 is open in the security groups configuration

Permissions in Redash

Not all data is meant to be viewed and edited by all users, and there are rare cases where we don't need to restrict the access to one or more resources in some way (except maybe proof-of-concept works, or garage-mode startups where everyone is an admin).

In this section, we will cover the permissions mechanism in Redash.

Groups

The core of Redash's permissions model are **Groups**.

Users are members of **groups**, while **Data Sources** are associated with **groups**.

Group membership by a user defines the actions they can perform, and the Data Sources they can access.

Each DataSource can be associated with one or more groups.

Currently, there are two types of relations between a DataSource and a group:

- **Full Access:** Members of this group can `create` and `run` new queries, as well as existing ones
- **Read Only Access:** Members of this group can only view existing queries and existing results

Each user can be a member of one or more Groups.

There is a default group, which was created with the installation of Redash, called `Default`.

Upon creation, every user becomes a member of the Default group. It's a good practice to associate the commonly used Data Sources with the Default group.

When creating a dashboard, you can mix whatever Data Sources you wish into queries, as long as you (the creating user) have access to them.

When a user who doesn't have access to some datasource (and hence to the visualization of that query), a dashboard will open with the restricted element – they will see only the placeholder, but won't be able to see its details.

 The general guideline – leverage the permissions mechanism of your underlying Data Sources as much as possible.

For example, if you want to restrict a user to a single table within a datasource, you need to do the following:

1. Create a separate user **in that datasource**, who only has access to the table you wish them to view.
2. Create a **datasource in Redash**, which uses the restricted user you've just created.
3. Create a new group and associate the datasource from step #2 with this group.
4. Add the user you wish to restrict to the group from step #3.

Creating and editing groups

In order to get to the Groups menu, you have to first click on **Settings**, then on **Groups**.

When you get to the **Groups** screen, you will see a list of existing groups as well as a **+ New Group** button that allows you to create a new group:

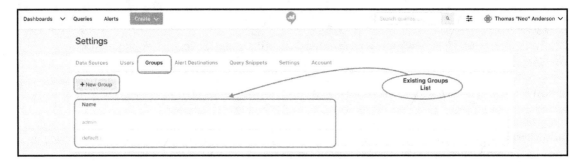

Let's create a new group called `test_group`.

To do so, click on the **+ New Group** button, and fill in the pop-up dialog with `test_group`.

This should take you to the new Group menu:

Now, you can add members (users) to the group, as well as associate Data Sources with the group.

Both adding new members and Data Sources features autocomplete in their edit boxes.

In the following screenshot, I try to add the user **alexander** to the `test_group`, and immediately after when I type the first letters, you can see the autocomplete in action:

In the following screenshot, you can see the **Data Sources** of the **default** group as a reference.

We can see that all of them are **Full Access**, which means that all the members of the default group can create and run new queries on those Data Sources:

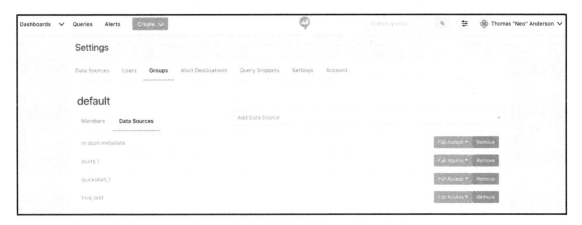

 You can't delete the **admin** and **default** groups

Creating users

 Creating new users can be done by **admins** (members of the **admin** group) only. In order to make a user an admin, simply add them to the **admin** group (on the **groups** menu).

To create a new user, click first on **Settings**, then on **Users** to get to the Users menu.

Inside the **Users** menu, click on the **+ New User** button:

For this example, we will create a new user named `Morpheous`.

Click on the **+New User** button and fill in the name and email of the new user:

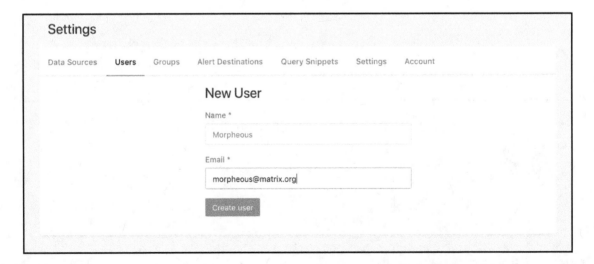

After filling in all the details, click on **Create User** and you should see the confirmation box where you can also find a `manual` invite link (in case you didn't set up the email properly, as shown in the following example):

Congratulations— you've just added another Redash user to the system!

Summary

In this chapter, we covered the different options of installing a self-hosted Redash, including detailed step by step guidance. We also reviewed the `setup.sh` script, which is the *basis* of all of the installation options, and went through a common troubleshooting practice.

Then, we covered how to configure and test emails, went over all of Redash's environment settings, and in addition covered the permissions mechanism (Users and Groups) in Redash.

The next chapter will guide you in how to create your first queries, visualizations, and dashboards.

3
Creating and Visualizing your First Query

This chapter is intended for the readers out there who are willing to go hands-on as soon as possible, and produce their first insights right away.

In this chapter, we will have a quick walk through the basic query visualization dashboard flow, to help you get started immediately.

This chapter's purpose is to do a quick overview of the common way to create queries and give you the necessary tools to digest data right away.

An in-depth overview of all the possible Data Sources / queries, and their creation and visualizations (as well as alerts), will be covered in the chapters that follow.

In this chapter, we will cover the following topics:

- Creating and testing the Data Source
- Creating your first query
- Creating your first visualization
- Creating your first dashboard

Creating and testing the Data Source

First, we need to define a Data Source. A Data Source is a place where our data resides; it can be an RDBMS (such as MySQL or Postgres), a comma-separated text file, a document store, and so on (these features will be covered in Chapter 4, *Connecting to Data Sources*).

For this chapter, we will be using Redash's internal PostgreSQL (the same example will work as is for any SQL queriable Data Source), to be able to execute parts of this specific example, you must have the dockerized PostgreSQL server set up.

 In case you don't have any Data Source set up yet, but you still wish to explore Redash and continue through this chapter, skip the PostgreSQL definition, and move to *Alternative Static Data Source Definition* right after it.

To validate that your dockerized PostgreSQL is up and running execute the following command:

```
docker ps
```

The output of the previous command should be similar to this:

CONTAINER ID	IMAGE	COMMAND	CREATED	STATUS	PORTS	NAMES
43f0ab719731	redash_worker	"/app/bin/docker-ent.."	4 days ago	Up 13 minutes	5000/tcp	redash_worker_1
dac9e681f48b	redash_server	"/app/bin/docker-ent.."	4 days ago	Up 13 minutes	0.0.0.0:5000->5000/tcp	redash_server_1
a9883a0fdb69	redis:3.0-alpine	"docker-entrypoint.s.."	4 days ago	Up 13 minutes	6379/tcp	redash_redis_1
68825b043ce1	postgres:9.5.6-alpine	"docker-entrypoint.s.."	4 days ago	Up 13 minutes	5432/tcp	redash_postgres_1

Details of the Data Source for this example are as follows (please note that in case you're using a non docker installation of redash, the `host` value in this example should be changed to the address of **your** PostgreSQL/MySQL database):

- Host: `redash_postgres_1`
- Port: `5432` (default)
- User name: `postgres`
- Database: `postgres`

 Before creating the Data Source, validate that Redash can access the Data Source server!

If you're not using the default dockerized PostgreSQL, then you might want to check that you have access to your target DB as in the following example, we will be using `telnet` to validate that PostgreSQL listens on port 5432 and that it's not firewalled.

Despite looking simple, this check eventually saves time, especially in secure environments with lots of firewall rules:

```
root@ip-10-69-10-45:/home/bitnami
root@ip-10-69-10-45:/home/bitnami
telnet 54.156.58.190 5432
Trying 54.156.58.190...
Connected to 54.156.58.190.
Escape character is '^]'.
^]
telnet>
```

After validating that our Postgres database is not firewalled, and listening on the desired port, we can move on and define this Data Source in Redash.

Click on the settings icon on the top right to get to the **Settings** screen, and then click on the **+New Data Source** button to create a new Data Source, as shown in the following screenshot:

On the **Data Sources** screen, select PostgreSQL and fill in the form with the necessary details:

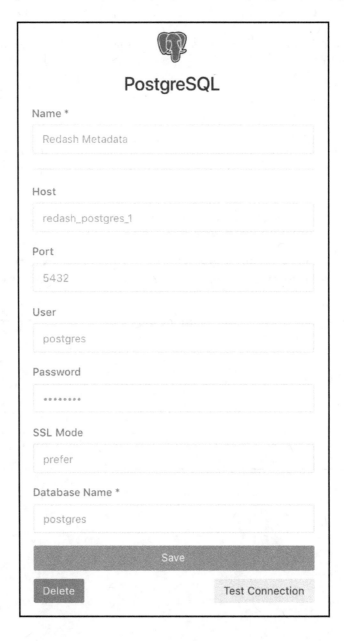

After filling in all the necessary fields for your Data Source, there is a very useful option to can test its connection.

Simply click on the **Test Connection** button, as follows:

Alternative static Data Source definition

The alternative Data Source is a URL Data Source (more details in `Chapter 4`, *Connecting to Data Sources*), and it holds the same ResultSet as the PostgreSQL Data Source presented previously. For convenience purposes, the name of this Data Source is `quickstart_1`.

Follow the same instructions as for PostgreSQL, but instead of PostgreSQL, select **Url** from the Data Sources options, and fill in the following details:

URL Base
Path: `https://raw.githubusercontent.com/PacktPublishing/Redash-Quick-Start-Guide/master/chapter3/sample_data/`

After you have saved the newly created Data Source (same for PostgreSQL and URL), we can proceed to writing our first query.

Creating your first query

Click on **Create** and select query from the drop-down menu. This will bring you to the query editor window, where the first thing you will have to select is the Data Source of the query (the Data Source selector is on the top-left-hand side of the window, right below **QueryName**, which in the case of creating a new query will be **New Query**). In this example, we will use one of the Data Sources we've just created (**Redash Meatadata** or **quickstart_1**):

After selecting the desired Data Source (in our case, **Redash Metadata**), we should see the schema (the available tables and their structure) on the left-hand side below the Data Source selector:

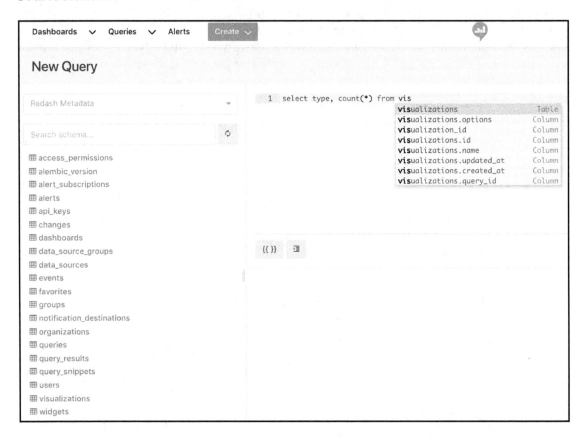

 Not all the Data Sources have schemas available.
If you used a URL Data Source, you won't see the schema.

We can then start typing our query into the query editor window (the main section right in the middle of the screen).

Autocomplete is available by default, and is presented automatically (unless we have lot of tables/columns, in which case you have to hit *Ctrl + Space*).

For the next example, we will use the **visualizations** table, which represents visualizations that are created in Redash.

The table has the following columns: **id, type, query_id, name, description, options, created_at, updated_at**.

In our example, the query is as follows (for SQLish datasources):

```
select type, count(*) from visualizations group by type order by count(*);
```

If you used our alternative URL Data Source, the query is as follows:

```
sample_url_datasource.json
```

This will show us the distribution of the visualization types.

After we have finished writing the query, we can execute it to see the results it returns:

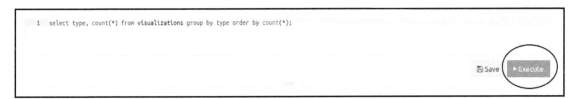

 A new query always starts in an **Unpublished** state, meaning that no one except you can see it. After saving the query, publish it to allow others to see it.

If you want to get a preview of the query results (and check whether this dataset is what you had in mind), click on the **Execute** button. Once you're happy with the query and the results, and you want to add a visualization, save the query.

After the query has finished executing, we can see the results in the form of a table right below the query window:

Table	+ New Visualization	
type		**count ▲**
TABLE		7,017
CHART		2,287
PIVOT		187
COUNTER		179
COHORT		150
MAP		128
SUNBURST_SEQUENCE		92
SANKEY		85
WORD_CLOUD		85
BOXPLOT		26

Edit Visualization   ‹› Embed   Download Dataset ▲   (10 rows 0 seconds runtime   Updated an hour ago)

At the bottom of the page, the following metadata will be present:

Row count, query runtime, and last update time.

Also note that after we save the query, it is possible to share it through a URL (in the form of `http://$REDASH_IP_OR_HOSTNAME/queries/$QUERY_ID`). In our example, the URL is `http://54.159.153.159/queries/5`, and if you open it, you should see the query results in the form of a table. If you want to edit the query, you need to click on **Edit Source**:

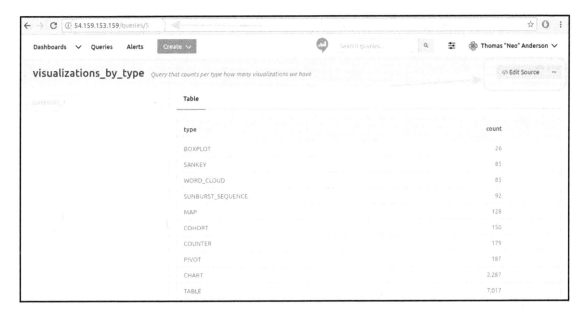

Creating the visualization

After we have saved the query (and given it a meaningful name instead of New Query; in our case, it's `visualizations_by_type`), we can create a visualization for it.

 The table with the query results inside it is also considered a visualization.

From within the query source (if you're not in query edit mode, click on **Edit Source**), click on **+New visualization**:

You will see the **Visualization Editor** window, where you can the **Visualization Type** (and optionally give your visualization a name):

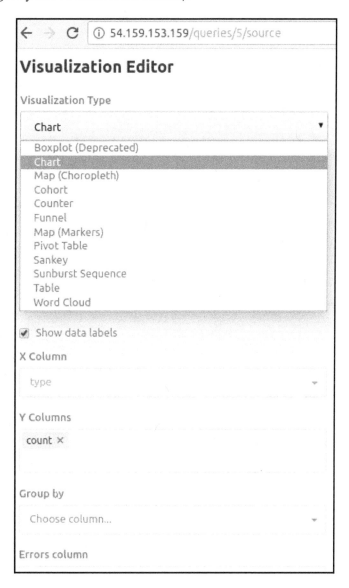

Here is an example of **Word Cloud**, which is a **Visualization Type** (as you can see, you only need to provide the column from which the **Word Cloud** is generated):

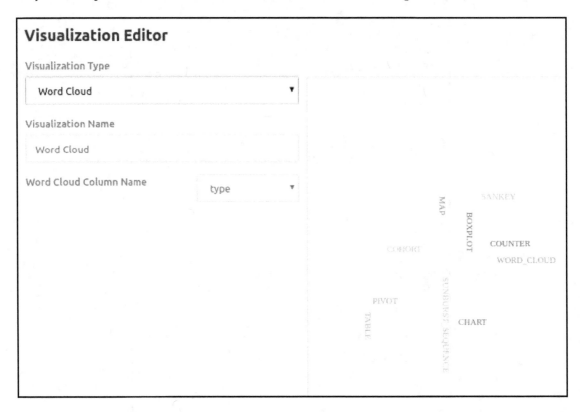

And here is a much more classic visualization of the chart. Note that this is in preview mode, so the visualization is changed automatically after you select a different type. However, it's not saved, so you still have to click **Save** at the end of the process:

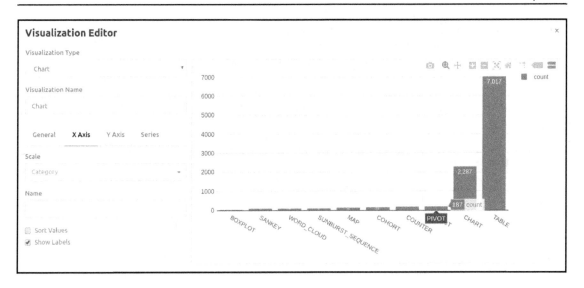

In the chart, there are more parameters that you have to set (such as the column type for the x and y axis, stacking, chart type, axes scale, and so on).

Starting at Redash v5, an **Auto Detect** scale feature was introduced, which means that Redash can now detect by itself the scale of values within the axes.

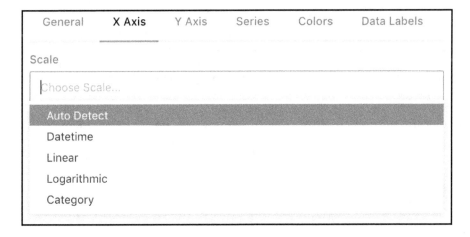

If you're using an older version of Redash, or if you do see results in the table, yet somehow the chart you've just added doesn't display any data, even though you added the right columns, there is a chance that the answer is hidden in a different scale type of the *x* or *y* axes.

A more in-depth overview of all the parameters of each visualization will be covered in Chapter 6, *Creating Visualizations*:

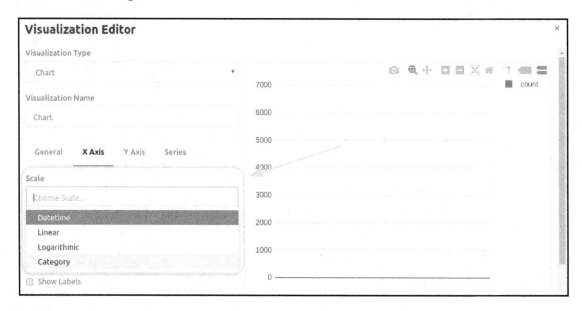

After we get our desired visualization, we have to click **Save** to add it to the query (and later to a dashboard).

Visualizations and queries are different entities, and you have to save them separately.

 It's a good practice to introduce a company-wide naming convention for queries/visualizations (and even dashboards); for example, a dashboard named **Marketing Daily Revenue Reports** or a query named **Bidding Platform Hourly Revenue**. It brings a lot of order, as opposed to generic names such as **test123** that can quickly pile up and cause user frustration.

After saving, you should see your new visualization along with the **Table** visualization in the query window:

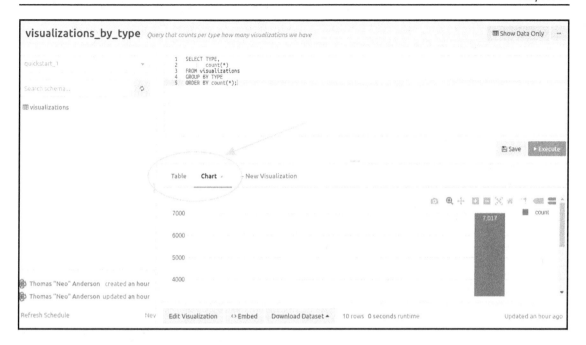

After validating that your new visualization has been added, we can move on to creating the dashboard.

Creating the dashboard

From the top menu, click on **Create** and choose **Dashboard**.

You will see a pop-up menu where you have to enter the dashboard's name (in this example, `quick dashboard` will be used as the dashboard's name):

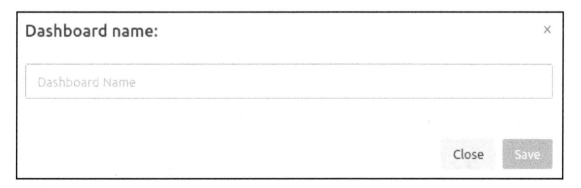

After filling in the name, you will get to a new dashboard window (which is also in an **Unpublished** state, meaning that only you can see it).

Click on **Add Widget** to start adding visualizations to this dashboard:

In the **Add Widget** window, we first need to select the query from which the results/visualizations will be taken, and afterwards we need to select the specific visualization itself (again, note that the table is also a visualization):

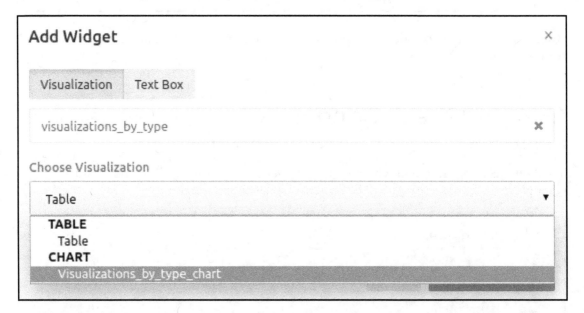

For this example, we add both **Table** and **Chart**, and the resulting dashboard will look like this:

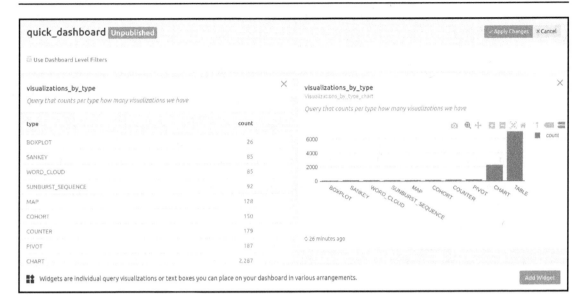

We can click on **Apply Changes** to save it.

Even though the dashboard is saved, it doesn't mean that everyone can see it; it's still in an unpublished state, so we need to publish it:

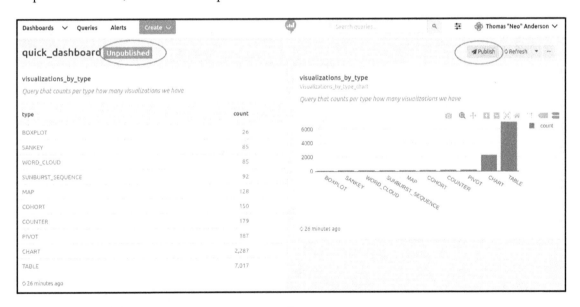

After clicking **Publish**, we can share the dashboard with others.

Summary

In this chapter, we covered the common process of creating a visualized query, starting from choosing and connecting to a Data Source, and then validating the connection. Afterward, we created the query and visualized it, and in the end added it to a dashboard.

The whole purpose of this chapter was to demonstrate the simplicity and the ease of use of Redash for digesting and visualizing your data. Based on the examples we covered in this chapter, you now have the initial tools to *demonstrate* Redash to your peers/managers.

The next couple of chapters will do a more thorough coverage of Data Sources, the query editor, and visualizations.

4
Connecting to Data Sources

To start querying your data, you first need to connect to a Data Source, as mentioned in brief in Chapter 3, *Creating and Visualizing your First Query*. The Data Source is where the data resides.

It can be a traditional database, .csv file, a brand new fancy NoSQL store, or even an existing query result!

Redash allows you to create running queries on top of all of them.

Please note that the terminology might be a bit confusing since, when saying Data Source, we might mean both the Data Source itself (not inside Redash, for example, an ElasticSearch cluster), and the *Redash Data Source,* which represents the connection from within Redash to the external Data Source. The surrounding context should help with overcoming this confusion.

In this chapter, we will be reviewing the various Data Sources in detail.

We will be covering the following topics:

- Supported Data Sources
- Adding a new Redash Data Source
- A detailed walkthrough Selected Data Sources
- The specific querying flavor of Data Sources

Supported Data Sources

Every business, especially a constantly growing business, has different data storage demands, and often they can't be fulfilled by a single Data Source. Although there are several Data Sources that can be considered *all-around* players (for example, PostgreSQL), there is no *silver bullet* that targets all needs, and it's not a rare case to see more than one Data Source in use.

The following is a real world example.

A company uses MySQL for financial transaction management, ElasticSearch is used to provide users with quick text search on their stored data, and Google Analytics is used to track their website metrics.

As of the current Redash version (version 5.0.0 at the time of writing this book), the following Data Sources are supported:

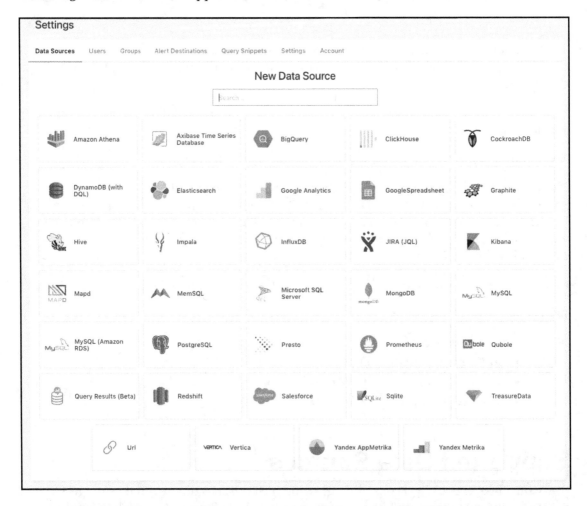

 Not all the supported Data Sources will be displayed all the time, since not all of the Data Sources have all their dependencies installed.

If you found that your desired Data Source is not in the list, it's about time to check the `requierements_all_ds.txt` and `requirements_oracle_ds.txt` files, and install the missing dependencies.

More on that in `Chapter 8`, *Customizing Redash*.

 The word *serverless* in the following context means that it's not you who manages the servers.

Cassandra, Oracle, SnowFlake, ScyllaDB, appmetrika, metrika

A word on each Data Source:

- **Amazon Athena**: An AWS serverless service that allows you to execute SQL like queries on data that resides on S3 (`https://aws.amazon.com/athena/`). Query language: SQL
- **Axibase Time Series Database**: A non-relational database that is optimized for temporal data collection and analysis (metrics) (`https://axibase.com/products/axibase-time-series-database/`). Query language: SQL
- **BigQuery**: Google's serverless, highly scalable, enterprise data warehouse (`https://cloud.google.com/bigquery/`). Query language: SQL
- **Cassandra:** Open source, distributed, wide column store initially developed at Facebook. Masterless design, provides high availability with no single point of failure (`http://cassandra.apache.org/`). Query language: CQL (SQL like)
- **ClickHouse**: Yandex's open source column-oriented DBMS, which is fault-tolerant and linearly scalable (`https://clickhouse.yandex/`). Query language: SQL

- **CockroachDB**: A distributed, horizontally scalable database based on the transactional and strongly consistent KV store (`https://www.cockroachlabs.com/`).
  Query language: SQL

- **DyanamoDB (with DQL):** An AWS serverless non-relational database that supports KeyValue and document store models (DQL is a special wrapper that allows executing SQL-like queries; `https://aws.amazon.com/dynamodb/`).
  Query language: SQL

- **ElasticSearch**: A distributed, RESTful search and analytics engine built on top of Lucene (`https://www.elastic.co/products/elasticsearch`).
  Query language: JSON

- **Google Analytics**: Google's web analytics service that tracks and reports website traffic (`https://developers.google.com/analytics/devguides/reporting/core/v4/`).
  Query language: JSON

- **GoogleSpreadSheet**: An online spreadsheet app that lets you create and format spreadsheets.
  (`https://www.google.com/sheets/about/`)
  Query language: Text

- **Graphite**: An open source tool that monitors and graphs numeric time series data.
  (`https://graphiteapp.org/`)
  Query language: Text

- **Hive**: Apache's data warehouse software project on top of Apache Hadoop.
  (`https://hive.apache.org/`)
  Query language: SQL

- **Impala**: Apache's, open source, distributed SQL query engine for Apache Hadoop.
  (`https://impala.apache.org/`)
  Query language: SQL

- **InfluxDB**: An open source time series DB platform for metrics and events.
  (`https://www.influxdata.com/`)
  Query language: SQL

- **JIRA (JQL):** A connector that allows you to run **JQL (Jira Query Language)** queries to fetch data from Atlassian's Jira (issue and project tracking software).
  (`https://confluence.atlassian.com/jiracore/blog/2015/07/search-jira-like-a-boss-with-jql`)
  Query language: Text (somewhat similar to SQL, but has specific syntax)

- **Kibana**: Outside of the Redash context, Kibana is a visualization tool for ElasticSearch. In the context of Redash, Kibana is just a different querying flavor of ElasticSearch. (`https://www.elastic.co/guide/en/kibana/current/lucene-query.html`)
  Query language: Text (Lucene querying syntax)
- **Mapd**: An open source relational, columnar SQL engine that was developed to harness GPU computing for real-time analytics (`https://www.mapd.com/`).
  Query language: SQL
- **MemSQL**: A distributed, in-memory, SQL database management system, compatible with MySQL (`https://www.memsql.com/`).
  Query language: SQL
- **Microsoft SQL Server:** Microsoft's RDBMS (`https://www.microsoft.com/en-us/sql-server/sql-server-2017`).
  Query language: SQL
- **MongoDB:** An open source document-oriented NoSQL datastore (`https://www.mongodb.com/`).
  Query language: JSON
- **MySQL/MariaDB**: The most popular open source DBMS (`https://mariadb.org/`), (`https://www.mysql.com/`).
  Query language: SQL
- **MySQL (Amazon RDS)**: The same as MySQL, but it has different connection parameters since it resides on AWS **Relational Database Service (RDS)** (`https://docs.aws.amazon.com/AmazonRDS/latest/UserGuide/CHAP_MySQL.html`).
  Query language: SQL
- **Oracle Database:** Multi-model DBMS made by Oracle, mostly used for running online transaction processing (OLTP), data warehousing (DW), and mixed (OLTP and DW) database workloads (`https://www.oracle.com/database/index.html`).
  Query Language: SQL
- **PostgreSQL**: An open source **ORDBMS (Object-Relational Database Management System)**, considered the most advanced open source database (`https://www.postgresql.org/`).
  Query language: SQL
- **Presto**: An open source distributed SQL query engine for running interactive analytic queries against Data Sources of all sizes, such as (but not limited to) Hive/Cassandra/Redis and so on (`https://prestodb.io/`).
  Query language: SQL

- **Prometheus**: An open source monitoring system with a dimensional data model, flexible query language, efficient time series database, and modern alerting approach (`https://prometheus.io/`).
  Query language: Text (specific prometheus syntax)
- **Qubole**: A self-service platform for big data analytics built on Amazon, Microsoft, Google, and Oracle clouds (`https://www.qubole.com/`).
  Query language: SQL
- **Query Results (Beta)**: Redash's option to treat any query result set as a new Data Source.
  Query language: SQL
- **Redshift**: An AWS severless massively parallel columnar storage analytical data warehouse.
  (`https://aws.amazon.com/redshift/`)
  Query language: SQL
- **Salesforce**: A connector that allows you to run SQL queries on Salesforce data using the **Salesforce Object Query language** (**SOQL**) (`https://developer.salesforce.com/docs/atlas.en-us.soql_sosl.meta/soql_sosl/sforce_api_calls_soql.htm`).
  Query language: SQL
- **ScyllaDB**: Open Source distributed NoSQL data store, designed to be compatible with Apache Cassandra and provide higher throughput and lower latencies.
  (`https://www.scylladb.com/`)
  Query language: CQL
- **SnowFlake:** Serverless Analytic Data Warehouse (`https://www.snowflake.com/about/`)
  Query language: SQL
- **Sqlite**: A self-contained, highly reliable embedded SQL engine (`https://www.sqlite.org/`).
  Query language: SQL
- **TreasureData**: Arm's cloud analytics and management platform for data (emphasis on data for the **Internet of Things** (**IoT**); `https://www.treasuredata.com/`).
  Query language: SQL

- **Url**: Redash's option to fetch data from any web-based source (a special format for this is needed, which is described in this chapter).
  Query language: None
- **Vertica**: A highly available, massively scalable, columnar storage analytical database platform, designed to provide fast query performance even on large volumes of data (`https://www.vertica.com/`).
  Query language: SQL
- **Yandex AppMetrika:** AppMetrica is a marketing platform for app install attribution, app analytics, and push campaigns (`https://appmetrica.yandex.com/`).
  Query language: SQL
- **Yandex Metrika:** All-Round Web Analytics including, but not limited to, traffic trends, mouse movements, ad campaigns, user analytics, and so on (`https://metrica.yandex.com/`) get a comprehensive understanding of your online audience and drive business growth.
  Query language: SQL

Adding a new Redash Data Source

To add a new Data Source, follow these steps:

1. Click on the settings icon in the top-right header:

2. On the settings page, under the **Data Sources** tab, click on the **+ New Data Source** button:

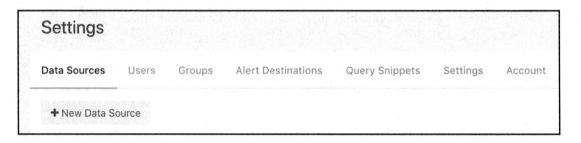

3. Select the desired Data Source from the displayed list, or start typing the Data Source name in the text box to filter the supported Data Sources list, and then select your Data Source from the narrowed list (in the following screenshot, we started typing `sql`, and you can see the filtered Data Sources that match the `sql` substring in regards to their names):

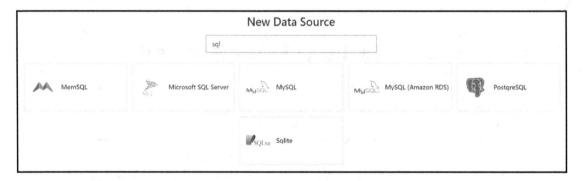

4. Fill in the necessary information about your Data Source.

All Data Sources can be used on a hosted Redash and a self-hosted Redash, except for Python (still in beta) Data Sources, which can only be used on a self-hosted Redash.

When using a hosted Redash, most of the time the traffic is firewalled, so you have to verify that the Redash server actually can connect to the Data Source (on the specific port of that Data Source; it's usually a simple rule in the firewall).

When possible, it is highly recommended to use a user with read-only permissions on the Data Source (the user that we use to let Redash connect to the Data Source).

 Don't forget to use the **Test Connection** button when creating the Data Source, as this saves a lot of time afterwards.

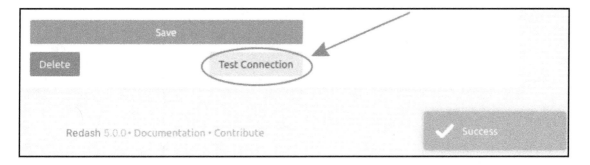

As explained previously, Redash supports many Data Sources. In this chapter, we will focus on PostgreSQL , ElasticSearch, MongoDB, GoogleSpreadsheet, Query Results (Beta), URL, Amazon Athena, BigQuery, Redshift, and DynamoDB (with DQL).

A detailed walk-through of the selected Data Sources

The aforementioned Data Sources represent the vast majority of the most frequently used Data Sources, and you can easily use the other Data Sources by using them as examples.

For instance, here we are covering a connector for PostgreSQL, and you can use it as a baseline for all of your SQL-based Data Sources, such as Vertica or MySQL.

For each of these Data Sources, we'll review and explain the Data Source fields that are used in setup (most of the fields should be self-explanatory).

Connecting to PostgreSQL

After selecting the PostgreSQL Data Source from the list, the PostgreSQL Data Source page is displayed and the user is prompted for the following information:

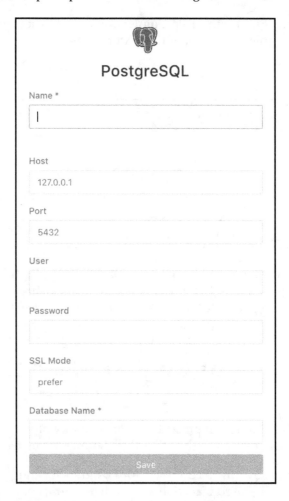

- **Name**: The Data Source name. The chosen name will be used in queries, dashboards, and so on.
- **Host**: The host name or IP address of your PostgreSQL server.
- **Port**: The port that PostgreSQL is listening to. The default PostgreSQL port is 5432.
- **User**: The username for the database.
- **Password**: The password for the preceding user field.

- **SSL Mode**: The value of SSL Mode determines the level of protection when connecting to the database. The default value for SSL Mode is `prefer`, which means that if SSL is available, the connection will use it; otherwise, the connection will be made without SSL. For further details, refer to the PostgreSQL manual or consult your DBA.

Connecting to ElasticSearch

There are two ElasticSearch flavors that are supported by Redash, and each has its own separate Data Source.

The first one is named **Kibana** and uses the Lucene querying syntax, and is widely used in Kibana (an open source ElasticSearch visualization platform).

The query syntax for the Kibana Data Source is text-based, and comes in the form of `field_name: value`.

The second one is named **ElasticSearch** and uses ElasticSearch's JSON-based querying syntax.

After selecting ElasticSearch/Kibana from the Data Sources list, the selected Data Source page is displayed, and the user is required to enter the following details (note the fields in both Data Sources are exactly the same – the only difference is in the querying engine):

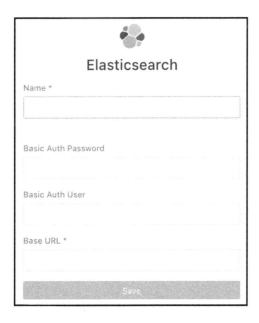

- **Name**: The chosen name of the Data Source.
- **Basic Auth Password**: The password for the database.
- **Basic Auth User**: The user for the database (that has the password specified in the preceding field).
- **Base URL**: The URL that consists of the protocol, host, and port of the ElasticSearch server `<PROTOCOL>://<HOST>:<PORT>`.
- The protocol is either HTTP or HTTPS (if there is an HTTPS proxy in front of ElasticSearch). The host is the host name or IP address of any node in the ElasticSearch server. The port that ElasticSearch is listening to is, by default, port `9200`.

Connecting to MongoDB

After choosing MongoDB from the Data Sources list, the MongoDB Data Source page will be displayed, and the user needs to enter the following connection information:

- **Name:** The Data Source name
- **Connection String**: The format of the connection string, that is, `mongodb://username:password@hostname:port/dbname?options`

We will describe the fields of the connection string shortly:

- The `username:password@` is optional. If given, the client will attempt to log in using these credentials to a database after connecting to the Mongo DB server.
- The port is the port that MongoDB is listening to. By default, the port is `27017`, unless specified otherwise.
- The `hostname` is the only required field in the connection string. This is the host name or IP address of the MongoDB server.
- The `dbname` is optional. This is the database name to authenticate when the connection string consists of the database credentials (`username:password field`).

> - **Note**: If `dbname` is not given in the connection string, but the credentials are specified, the client will authenticate to the admin database using those credentials.

- `?options` are connection-specific options. The options are specified in the form of name-value pairs. Pairs are seperated by `&`. For example, a connection string with enabled SSL and self-signed certificates is as follows: `mongodb://username:password@hostname:port/dbname?ssl=true&ssl_cert_reqs=CERT_NONE`.

- For more details and options, please refer to the MongoDB documentation.
- **Database Name:** The name of the database to log in to. The database name is also included in the connection string, although it is optional. A separated field for the database name is usually required when using shared hosts.
- **Replica Set Name:** The name of the replica set (in case your MongoDB is set up in production deployment, you should have replica sets for redundancy and high availability).

Connecting to GoogleSpreadsheet

- **Name:** The Data Source name
- **JSON Key File**: The JSON key file that was generated when the Google service account was created, and the path to the JSON key file

We will explain how to generate a Google service account and the corresponding **JSON key file*** shortly.

Here is how to create a Google Service Account:

1. Open the `Service accounts page`. If prompted, select a project.
2. Click **Create Service Account** at the top of the page.
3. In the **Create Service Account** window, type a name for the service account, and select **Furnish a New Private Key**. When prompted, select the JSON key file type. Then, click **Create**.

Connecting to Url

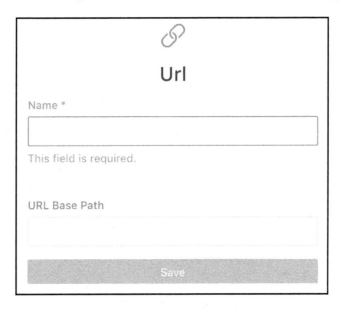

- **Name:** The Data Source name
- **URL Base Path**: The location of the desired file, starting with the host name and then the file address (without the filename and ending with a /)

Using a URL-based Data Source requires that the service that returns data on the specified URL will use our data format (see the following example).

The query itself inside Redash will simply contain the URL to be executed (such as `http://myserver/path/myquery`) and return with all the data it has.

Here's a list of valid column types that are acceptable to be returned in results:

- Integer
- Float
- Boolean
- String
- Datetime
- Date

To post-process the data you get from your URL Data Source, you have to save the query and then query that dataset (more about querying Query Results as Dataset is, covered later in this chapter).

The following is an example JSON that is expected to receive the URL from the Data Source:

```
{
   "columns": [
      {
         "name": "created_date",
         "type": "date",
         "friendly_name": "created_date"
      },
      {
         "name": "adv_uuid",
         "type": "string",
         "friendly_name": "advertiser_uuid"
      },
      {
         "name": "cmp_cnt",
         "type": "integer",
         "friendly_name": "campaigns_count"
      },
      {
         "name": "total_rev",
         "type": "double",
         "friendly_name": "total_revenue"
      }
   ],
   "rows": [
      {
         "adv_uuid": "518ff4e6-80ab-11e8-adc0-fa7ae01bbebc",
         "cmp_cnt": 50,
         "total_rev": 100.2,
         "created_date": "2018-05-30"
      },
      {
         "adv_uuid": "518334e6-80ac-22e8-ebc0-fa9ae011bc12",
         "cmp_cnt": 12,
         "total_rev": 2600.5,
         "created_date": "2018-02-01"
      }
   ]
}
```

As we can see in the preceding example, `columns` contain the column names and their datatypes, and `rows` contain the data itself.

Connecting to Query Results (beta)

The **Query Results** Data Source allows you to run queries on top of existing query results, so you can easily merge/refine results or perform any other kind of post-processing on the result set you already have:

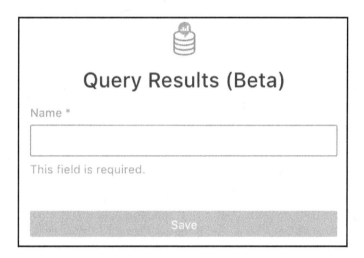

- **Name**: The name you wish to give to your Data Source

The naming convention when dealing with a Query Results Data Source is in the form of `query__$QUERY-ID`, where `$QUERY-ID` is the ID of your initial query that you wish to reuse the results of (that is, the number in the query URL).

For example, suppose your query is `http://demo.redash.io/queries/7177`. When referencing its results, you will use `query__7177` as the table name.

By referencing the table after creating the Data Source (for example, `query_555` and `query_666`), you will be able to execute queries like the following:

```
SELECT q1.name, q2.count FROM query_555 q1 JOIN query_666 q2 ON q1.id =
q2.id
```

 For this Data Source, you need to make sure that, when creating queries, the table name (for example, `query_123`) is on the same line as the FROM/JOIN keywords.

There are a few notes to consider:

- In order to keep the query results as fresh as possible, the source queries (the queries that you use as the Data Source) are also being executed every time you run a query on this Data Source. This might be changed in the future to reduce the number of concurrent executing queries and repeated query runs.
- The underlying engine that allows processing on this kind of Data Source is an in-memory SQLite database, so in case of operating with large datasets, you might hit an **OOM (Out of Memory)** error.
- **Access Control**: As mentioned in #1, the source query is also being executed during the execution of the resulting query, and so the user that is executing it must have access and the right to execute on both the query and the source query. If they don't have the right to access or execute, the user will be able to see the query but not execute it.

Connecting to Amazon Athena

To access Amazon Athena through Redash, you need to create an IAM user, if you haven't already. This user must have permissions to run queries with Amazon Athena and access S3 buckets that contain your data:

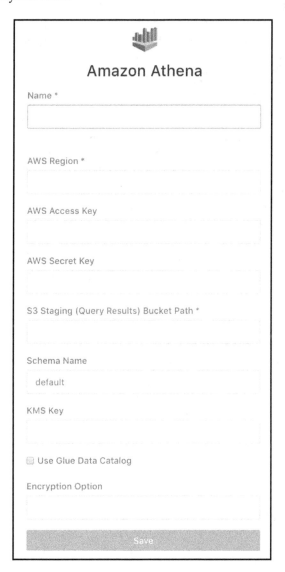

- **Name**: The Data Source name.
- **AWS Region**: The region of your Amazon Athena.
- **AWS Access Key**: The AWS Access Key from the Amazon account you created (to create new keys, see the AWS documentation).
- **AWS Secret Key**: The AWS Secret Key from the Amazon account you created (to create new keys, see the AWS documentation).
- **S3 Staging (Query Results) Bucket Path**: The path to the bucket that is used for the staging/query results.
- **Schema Name** (default): The name of the schema that will be used.
- **KMS Key**: The Key Management Service key. The optional values are ARN or ID.
- **Use Glue Data Catalog**: A checkbox that allows the user to select whether to use the Glue Data Catalog or not. The glue data catalog is a central metadata repository that stores metadata information about databases and tables, pointing to a data store in Amazon S3 or a JDBC-compliant data store.
- **Encryption Option**: Specifies the encryption option to use. The three optional values are as follows:
    - SSE-S3 (S3 server-side encryption with Amazon S3 managed keys)
    - SSE-KMS (server-side encryption with KMS-managed keys)
    - CSE-KMS (client-side encryption with KMS-managed keys)

Connecting to BigQuery

In order to set up a **BigQuery** Data Source in Redash, you need to create or already have a Google service account with permissions to access BigQuery. If you are creating a new service account, in the new private key generation, make sure that you select the JSON key file type, as it is required in the Data Source setup in Redash.

BigQuery uses **Identity and Access Management** (**IAM**) to manage access to resources. If you create a custom role, grant the role the following list of permissions:

- `bigquery.jobs.create`
- `bigquery.jobs.get`
- `bigquery.jobs.update`
- `bigquery.datasets.list`
- `bigquery.datasets.get`
- `bigquery.tables.list`

- `bigquery.tables.get`
- `bigquery.tables.getData`

Alternatively, you can use the predefined admin role in BigQuery:

- **Name**: The Data Source name.
- **Project ID**: Your BigQuery project ID. To get the ID of the project, go to the Google Cloud Platform Console and check the ID listed in the project info card.
- **JSON Key File**: The JSON Key file from the service account generation.
- **Load Schema**: When checked (checkbox), this allows the user to specify a table's schema when loading data into a table and when creating an empty table.
- **Use Standard SQL**: To enable Standard SQL, mark this checkbox.

- **Scanned Data Limit (MB)**: Limits the number of bytes scanned.
- **Maximum Billing Tier:** Limits the billing tier. Queries that use resources beyond this limit will fail.
- **UDF Source URIs (such as Gs://bucket/date Utils.js, Gs://bucket/string Utils.js)**: The URI for the **user-defined function (UDF)**. BigQuery supports executing UDFs over the BigQuery data. A UDF can be implemented by using another SQL statement or another programming language, such as JavaScript.

Connecting to Redshift

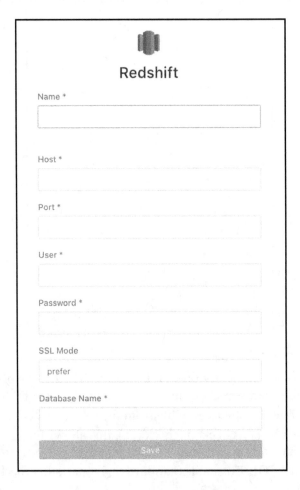

- **Name**: The Data Source name.
- **Host**: The host name or IP address of your Redshift server.
- **Port**: The port that Redshift is listening to. The default Redshift port is `5439`, but it might be different in order to enhance security.
- **User**: The username for the database.
- **Password**: The password for the preceding **User** field.
- **SSL Mode:** `prefer`; Redshift supports SSL connections. The default value for SSL Mode is `prefer`, which means that if SSL is available, the connection will use it, otherwise the connection will be made without SSL. As Redshift supports SSL, SSL is used when SSL Mode is set to prefer. For additional SSL Mode values, refer to the Redshift manual or consult your DBA.
- **Database Name**: The database name to log in to.

Connecting to DynamoDB

To query AWS DynamoDB, you have to use their own specific query language (not very intuitive to ordinary data analysts). Here in Redash, we use DQL, the **DynamoDB Query language**, an SQL-like language to query DynamoDB (you can read more about DQL here: `http://dql.readthedocs.io/en/latest/`).

To access DynamoDB through Redash, you must have an AWS access key and secret key, which are used to sign programmatic requests that you make to AWS.

If you don't have the desired keys, you can create them from the AWS Management Console. The keys can only be viewed and downloaded upon creation, and cannot be recovered later. You can create new access keys at any time:

- **Name**: The Data Source name
- **Access Key**: The AWS Access Key from the Amazon account you created (to create new keys, see the AWS documentation)
- **Region (us-east-1)**: The region of your Amazon DynamoDB (us-east-1 is the default in Redash)
- **Secret Key**: The AWS Secret Key from the Amazon account you created (to create new keys, see the AWS documentation)

Summary

In this chapter, we've covered the Data Sources section of Redash, showed off a large variety of Data Sources that Redash currently supports, explained in brief what each Data Source is, covered the process of adding a new Data Source, and performed a deep dive into a selected set of ten Data Sources that are used the most.

In the upcoming chapter, we will be covering querying itself, working with the result set, and diving into Redash's query editor.

Writing and Executing Queries

5

After connecting Redash to our Data Sources, we will advance to the next important milestone – writing the queries.

The purpose of Redash is to provide the team with a powerful tool to unleash the full potential of data analysis, and being able to quickly and easily write queries for multiple Data Sources across multiple teams and company verticals is a core value to reaching that milestone.

In this chapter, we will cover the following topics:

- Query listing
- Query editor overview
- Query operations (create, edit, fork, archive, and scheduling)
- Query results and filters
- Parametrized queries
- Query snippets
- Alerts

Query listing

To view the existing queries, click on the **Queries** option on the top menu. You will get to the **Queries** screen:

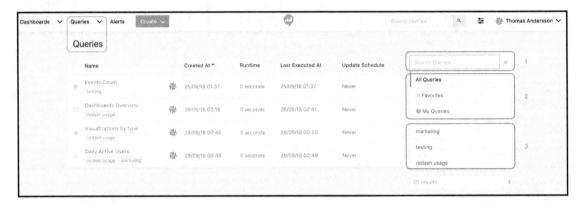

In the **Queries** screen, you will be able to view the list of all the queries that the current user is allowed to see. There is an option to narrow the list to more specific queries using the following:

1. **Search Box:** Just start typing and the list of queries will comply to your search pattern. **The search pattern applies to the query text as well**, so for example, if you don't remember the query name, but you do recall the table it queries - the search will find your query.
2. **All Queries / Favourites / My Queries**: This toggles between the list of All the queries / only starred queries / only queries created by the current user.
3. **Tags**: This filters the queries by specific tag.

In the following image, we see all the queries tagged with the **redash usage** tag.

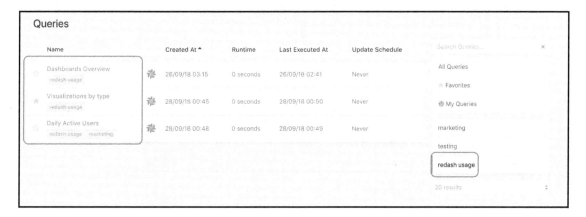

Query editor overview

To get to the query editor, either click on **Create – New Query** or click on an existing query (like the ones you found in the previous paragraph).

Let's look at an overview of all the components of the query editor:

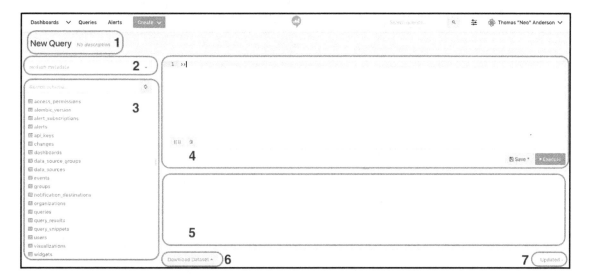

1. **Metadata**: This is the Query name, Tags, and Star (indicator of Favourite query).
2. **Data source selector**: Here, we choose where the query takes the data from (refer to chapter on Data Sources, for more detail).
3. **Schema browser**: This displays all the tables in the selected Data Source. The schema auto-refreshes periodically in the background, unless the user explicitly clicks on the **refresh schema** button. When clicking on a specific table, the schema expands to display its columns. In the upper part of the schema browser, you have the search box, which is where you can refine the schema according to the text you type. Clicking on the double arrow on the right-hand side of the selected schema entity will insert the clicked entity into the query editor:

In the case of large schemas (that have thousands of entities), the reload of the schema might take some time.

Not all of the Data Sources have the `get_schema` method implemented, which means that those who miss it will not display anything in the schema browser.

4. **Query Editor**: This is where you actually write your queries. Every Data Source has its own SQL (query language) flavor, but most of them try to be SQL-like. Auto complete is supported and automatically triggered when you start typing, unless your schema is really large (> 5,000 tokens), and then you have to trigger it manually with *Ctrl* + Spacebar.

   In addition, there is an option to format the SQL code (it brings the sql query to a more readable format):

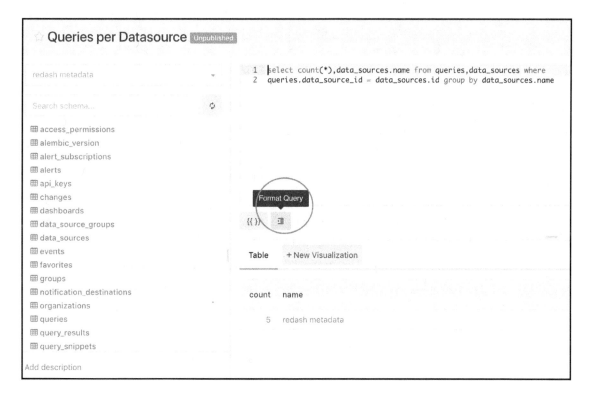

5. **Results and visualizations panel**: When you run your query, the results are displayed here, as well as any additional visualizations that you add to it.

6. **Results data menu**: The post execution menu allows you to download the dataset, get the code that embeds your visualization into an external resource, such as a website (through iframe), and edit visualizations for the query.

7. **Last update Information**: Here is the information about the last time the query ran.

Query operations

Redash offers a convenient way for working on your queries (yep, it's not just writing the query in the editor or pasting it from the Stack Overflow) in the form of operations. These operations can – and will – save you time when dealing with multiple queries over multiple Data Sources, and in collaboration between several teams. We will cover the core operations it offers in the following subsections.

Creating a query

To create a query, we can click on **Create** | **Query** from the top menu, which will take us to the create the **New Query** screen.

For this example, we will be using Redash's internal Data Source, called Redash metadata.

Select it using the Data Source selector (element #2 in the query editor overview chapter), and you should see that the Schema Browser refreshes with the updated schema (element #3 in the query editor overview chapter).

Now, let's create a simple query to see all the dashboards that are available in the system (without modifying anything else, and without saving anything, just to get a feeling of how it works).

Type `select * from dashboards` in the query editor window (element #4 in query editor overview chapter), and click on the **Execute** button.

We should now see that the query executes and returns results into the results visualization panel (element #5). The **Results Data** menu (element #6) and **Last Updated Info** (#7) should also be updated now:

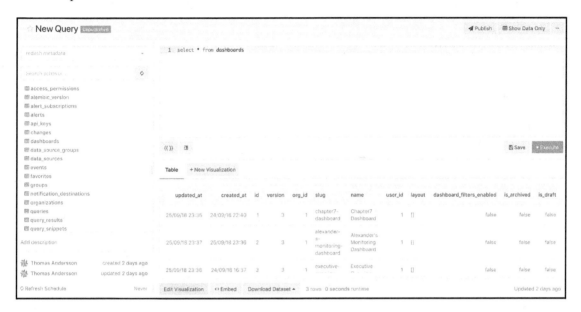

We've seen how the query executes and how the results are displayed, suppose we've decided that we need to do something different, like check how many queries there are per Data Source. Let's change the query to fetch what we need, and change the query name to something more meaningful (as well as the query description).

So, the new query is (note the join to bring the Data Source name instead of **id**) as follows:

```
select count(*),data_sources.name from queries,data_sources where
queries.data_source_id = data_sources.id group by data_sources.name
```

We have changed the query name to **Queries per Datasource** and the description to **Number of queries per Datasource**. Click on **Format SQL** (inside the query editor window) to arrange the SQL in a more convenient way.

Click on **Execute** to validate that the query we wrote doesn't have syntax errors and that we have the data that we need.

Then, click on **Save** to save the query. You should be able to get the following notification that your query was saved successfully:

Note the text **Unpublished** next to the query name, as well as the **Publish** button on the right-hand part of the screen.

There are two states for a saved query: **Published** and **Unpublished**. By default, the query starts as **Unpublished** (right after you save it for the first time).

An **Unpublished** state means that no one can see the query except the user who has created it (in All queries/my queries or search results). In addition, this means that you can't include unpublished query visualizations in dashboards, or use that query in alerts.

In order to move the query into a Published state, simply click on the **Publish** button on the right-hand part of the screen (don't worry – you can always unpublish in the same manner whenever you wish).

Clicking on the star (to the left of the query name) will add the query to favourites (we can filter favourite queries in the Query Listing page)

Clicking on +**Add tag** (to the right of the query name) will open a pop-up menu where we can add tags for queries. The usage of tags is similar to #hashtags on the internet, and we can later filter queries by tags, for easier and faster access to the desired query.

The Star and Tag options are depicted in the following image:

Useful keyboard shortcuts:

Ctrl/Cmd + S: Saves the query
Ctrl/Cmd + Enter: Executes the query

Editing a query

To edit a query, first, you need to find the query that you want to edit. There are several ways you can do this:

1. **Find the query through the query page**: Go to **Queries** and then you will be able to see it either in All Queries, My Queries, or in the Search menu.
2. **Find the query through a dashboard**: Click on the Widget that you want to find the query for, and you will get to the query page.
3. **Direct link**: A colleague might actually simply send you a direct link to the query (for example, for Redash, this is located at `demo.redash.io`; the query can be found at `http://demo.redash.io/queries/719`).

 The `query_id` is actually part of the URL, so in case you know the `query_id` in advance, you can find it at `https://www.your_redash.com/queries/query_id`.

After you find your desired query, you can click on **Edit Source** to edit the query:

The **Edit** menu looks the same as the **Create** menu.

However, if the query is not created by you, you might want to fork a query instead.

Forking a query

Forking (cloning or duplicating) a query is a concept that might be familiar to GitHub (and similar) users. It's an easy way to take an existing query (with all the surrounding settings) and duplicate it.

Forking comes in a variety of handy use cases; consider the following examples:

- The same query on a different Data Source (for comparison)
- The same basic query but with different boundary conditions (for example, monthly/weekly)
- A complex query that was written by a colleague that now needs to be adapted to your specific needs

In order to fork a query, you need to find the query you need to fork, and click on its menu:

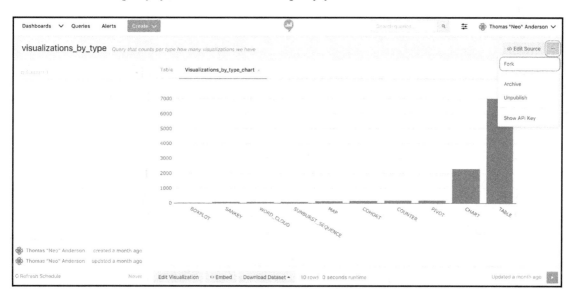

After clicking on **Fork** in the menu, you will get a duplicate of the query you forked.

The first thing you will notice is the change of query_id in the URL (http://your_redash_url/queries/new_query_id/source).

In addition to this, the new query will be in an Unpublished state, and the name will be Copy of (#`query_id`) where `query_id` is the ID of the query you forked:

Now, you can modify the query, change the Data Source, change the name, and so on.

Then, you can publish the query and use it in dashboards.

Archiving a query

There is no real delete in Redash, instead, when you feel that the query is no longer needed, and it just occupies space in the queries list, you can archive it.

From the users perspective, archiving is almost the same as deleting, since the visualizations of this query will be removed from dashboards.

The only difference is that archived queries will still be reachable through direct links (the URL of the query).

To archive a query, choose **Archive** from the query menu:

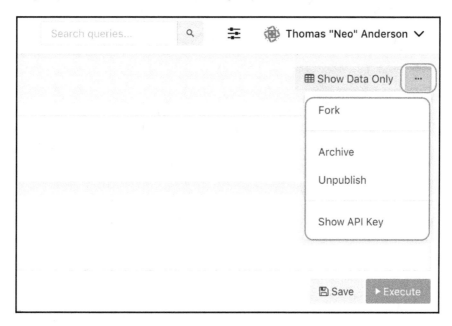

After you choose **Archive**, Redash will ask you if you're sure that you want to archive the query.

Click on **Archive** if you're sure, or on **Cancel** otherwise:

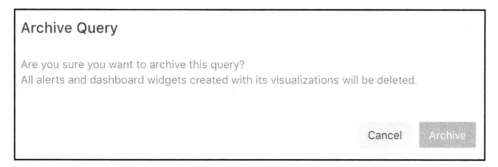

Now, your query won't appear in the queries list, and all the dashboard visualizations of it will be deleted.

If you have a direct URL of the query, however, you will be able to see it (with **Archived** next to its name):

Scheduling a query

The default for every newly created query is no scheduling, meaning that it only runs when you click on **Execute**.

Obviously, that scenario is not good for non-static dashboards, such as dashboards that can be used for monitoring. There, we would like to have auto-refresh enabled.

To do this, we must enable scheduling for the query.

When you locate the query you wish to schedule, look at the bottom left part to find the scheduling information:

The **Never** word is clickable, and will show you the scheduling popup (titled **Refresh Schedule**), which has two selectors. One says **No Refresh** and the other has a time selection option:

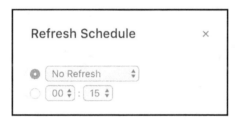

There are two scheduling options:

- Once a day, at specific time
- Every X minutes (hours, days)

If we want periodical scheduling, click on the **No Refresh** option, and you will see a pop-up menu of all the possible intervals:

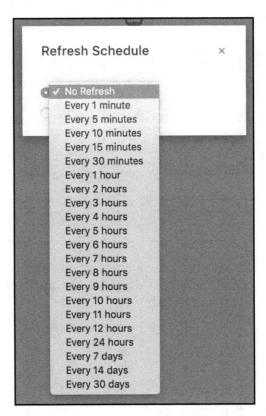

If you want a specific time once a day, select the clock option, and set it to the hour you wish.

For example, in the following screenshot, I set the query to run once a day at **01:25** (1:25 AM). The time zone is the time zone of the computer where Redash runs:

After the scheduler is set, Redash will execute that query automatically according to your settings.

 Parametrized scheduled queries will use default values when performing the scheduled run.

Query results and filters

Due to the very dynamic nature of business analysts nowadays, you often want to post-process query results in place, or download them and process them in your other-favorite-tool, or just simply email the results as a `csv` file to an external client.

Redash's query editor allows you to perform these actions right after the query returns its results.

Query results

It is possible to download the query results in various formats (`csv`, `json`, or `xslx`).

There are several ways to do this.

The first, and most trivial way, is to use the results data menu (element #6), which is located right below the query results window:

Click on the **Download Dataset**, and then you can select whether you want to download a CSV or an Excel file.

The other way is to click on the query's advanced menu, and choose **Show API Key:**

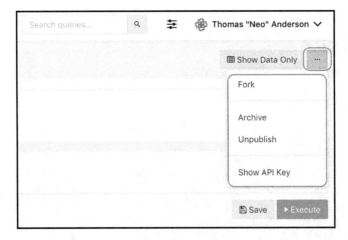

When clicking on **Show API key**, a pop-up menu will display showing the API key for the query, as well as URLs to download the query result set as JSON or CSV.

If you replace the file extension in the URLs you find there to XSLX, you will download the results in Excel format.

> The download dataset option always links to the query results that you see on the screen now, meaning that they can be outdated (for example, in case you left the query in a separate tab without refreshing).
> To get the most updated results in relation to the query, always refer to the URLs that are presented through the **Show API Key** option.

Query filters

Redash offers a simple and handy way to add filters to results and visualizations.

Suppose you have a query that shows the distribution of Redash users per country, and you want to filter the result to see only a specific country (or countries) without having to rewrite the query (because you do need the whole output for all countries).

It is possible to do exactly that with filters!

Redash offers two types of filters:

- **Single value filter**: This means that you can select only a single value for the column you want to filter on
- **Multi value filter**: This means that you can have multiple values for the column you filter on

> You can have several filters on different columns in a single query.

In order to enable filters, you have to follow a specific naming convention.

Inside your query, you must add an *alias* to the column you want to filter on:

- `<column_name>::filter`: For a single value filter
- `<column_name>::multi-filter`: For a multi-value filter

In case your Data Source doesn't allow double colons (`::`) in the alias, you can use `__filter` and `__multiFilter` instead.

Since you're adding filter as an alias, don't forget to enclose it in double quotes! For example, `SELECT country AS "country::filter" FROM my_table`.

Let's look at an example. Suppose we have the following query:

```
SELECT type,
 count(*) AS count_per_type
FROM visualizations
GROUP BY type
ORDER BY count_per_type
```

This query returns the visualization type and the number of visualizations of that specific type. Now, I would like to make the type filtered.

I can modify the query, as follows:

```
SELECT type AS "visualization_type::filter",
 count(*) AS count_per_type
FROM visualizations
GROUP BY type
ORDER BY count_per_type
```

After you execute the query, you will be able to see the filter inside the results frame:

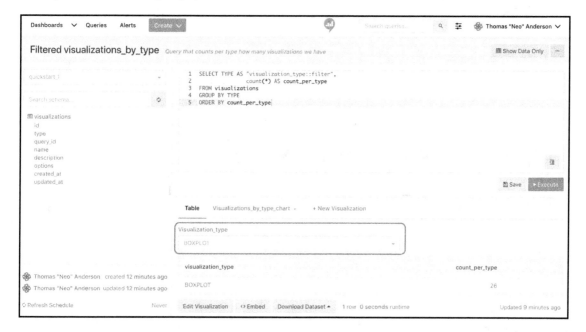

If you click on the filter, the slide menu with all the possible **visualization_types** will pop up, and you will be able to change the filter to another value.

The query is not being executed again; the filter is only on the end results:

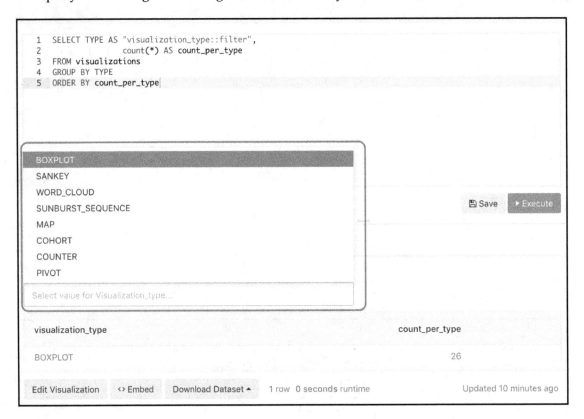

```
1   SELECT TYPE AS "visualization_type::filter",
2              count(*) AS count_per_type
3   FROM visualizations
4   GROUP BY TYPE
5   ORDER BY count_per_type
```

BOXPLOT
SANKEY
WORD_CLOUD
SUNBURST_SEQUENCE
MAP
COHORT
COUNTER
PIVOT

Select value for Visualization_type...

💾 Save   ▶ Execute

visualization_type	count_per_type
BOXPLOT	26

Edit Visualization   ‹› Embed   Download Dataset ▲   1 row 0 seconds runtime   Updated 10 minutes ago

If you download the dataset, you will have all the data, and not only the filtered columns, the filter is only representational!

Here is an example of a multi-filter, where you can select more than one value:

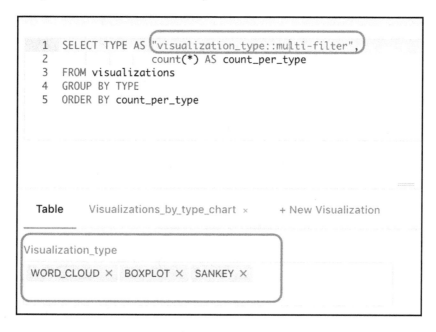

```
1   SELECT TYPE AS "visualization_type::multi-filter",
2                  count(*) AS count_per_type
3   FROM visualizations
4   GROUP BY TYPE
5   ORDER BY count_per_type
```

Table   Visualizations_by_type_chart ×   + New Visualization

Visualization_type

WORD_CLOUD ×   BOXPLOT ×   SANKEY ×

Parametrized queries

When there is a need to dynamically provide conditions (or any predicates, in fact) to the query, without having to rewrite it every time the conditions change, you know that you need query parameters.

Every query can be parametrized, and as we have already seen in filters, there is a convention for this.

Starting Redash v5, there are two ways to add a parameter to your query.

Either you add a keyword that is enclosed in double curly braces, for example, {{param_name}} to your query, and it will automatically introduce a parameter (exactly the same way as it was before v5 release).

Alternatively, you can click on the **Add New Parameter** button (shortcut **Cmd** / *Ctrl* + *P*).

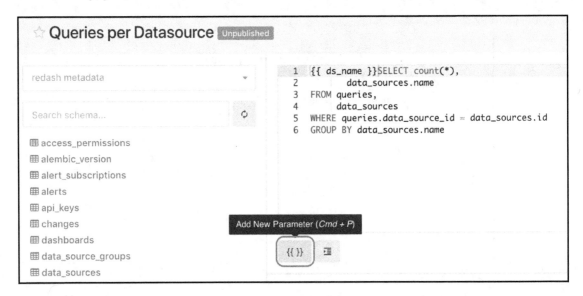

Once Redash recognizes that you've added a parameter, a special param box will appear in the query editor:

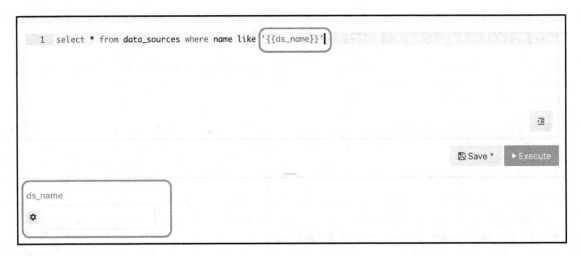

For example, in the preceding query, a parameter named '{{ds_name}}' was added, and right after Redash recognized it (we didn't have to execute or save the query for this to happen; it happens as you type), it added the param box on the bottom left of the query editor.

Now, you can enter your desired value in that param box, click on **Execute**, and see the results based on the value you entered.

In the preceding query example, the match on the *name* field would be exact. If you want a partial match, you can modify the query to be the following (%%, which wraps the param name, acts as a wildcard in SQL):

```
select * from data_sources where name like '%{{ds_name}}%'
```

> It is possible to use the same parameter several times in the query (if needed).
>
> It is also possible to create more than one parameter in a single query.

Parameter settings

Parameters in Redash have editable settings. In order to get to the settings menu, you have to click on the settings icon in the param box:

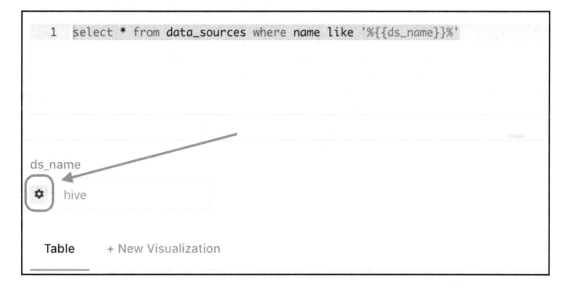

Once clicked, it will open a **Parameter Settings** menu, where you can control the title, type of parameter, and set whether it's **Global.** We will explain all of these settings shortly:

- **Title**: By default, it's just the param name that you gave it in the query, but you can always change it to something more meaningful for others (and for yourself).
- **Type**: The data type of the parameter (also affects the behavior of the param box UI). Its currently available types are **Text, Number, Dropdown List, Query Based Dropdown List, Date, Date and Time, Date**, and **Time** (with seconds), **Date Range, Date and Time Range, Date and Time Range** (with seconds). The Date Ranges - were introduced starting v5in addition with the support for Now/Today as default value of Date/Time parameter type.
- **Global**: When set (checkbox), the same parameter can be shared across multiple queries (the parameter in those queries must have the same name, and marked in all the queries as global). If not set, every query has its own parameter, even if the parameters have the same name!

Currently, parameters only work in manually executed queries – you can't have parametrized queries embedded elsewhere or in shared dashboards.

 In order to create and use parameters in a query, you must have Full Access permissions on the Data Source of the query.

Query snippets

Query snippets are parts of a query that often repeat themselves, and hence can be reused.

For example, a join between tables, a large `where [not] in`, or simply a frequently used constraint.

Use of the query snippets is time-saving, since now you can autocomplete large pieces of SQL code in seconds, and it can be shared between colleagues.

To create query snippets, go to **Settings | Query snippets:**

On the query snippets screen, you will see all the previously created snippets.

Click on the **+New Snippet** button to start creating a new snippet.

The new query snippet page is displayed and the following fields need to be filled in:

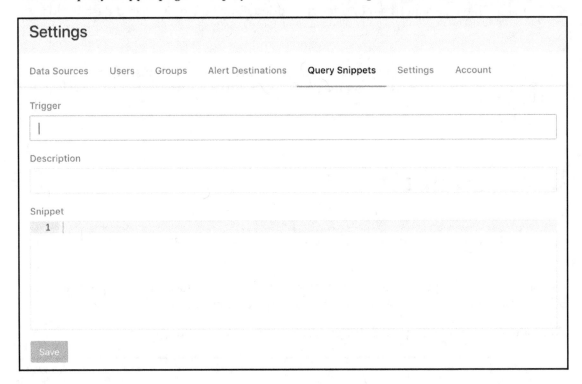

Trigger: This is the word that will be used to invoke the query snippet. The query editor will suggest auto-completion for this word when the user starts to type in the first few letters.

Description: This includes several words to describe the query snippet.

Snippet: This is where the user types the query snippet code.

Let's look at a quick example. Suppose I have the following query (outputs visualization types and count per type):

```
SELECT TYPE,
  COUNT(*)
FROM visualizations
GROUP BY TYPE
ORDER BY COUNT(*);
```

We will create a snippet from the `GROUP BY TYPE ORDER BY COUNT(*)` part.

Fill in all the fields as described previously with the following:

- Trigger will be **group_type_cnt**
- **Description**: The group by type and order by count snippet test (this field is not mandatory and can be left blank)
- **Snippet**: `GROUP BY TYPE ORDER BY COUNT(*)`

After we save the snippet, let's write our query again, but this time we can autocomplete the snippet part by starting to type its *trigger word*:

```
1   SELECT TYPE,
2          count(*)
3   FROM visualizations
4   gr
    group_type_cnt              snippet   group_type_cnt
    grant                       keyword
    group                       keyword
    integer                     keyword   GROUP BY TYPE ORDER BY count(*);
    ORG_ID_SNIPPET: ORG_ID_SNIPPET  snipp…
```

We can see that the autocomplete finds the snippet (and even marks its type as snippet). When we select it, it will simply insert the snippets code into our query – fast and easy:

```
1   SELECT TYPE,
2          count(*)
3   FROM visualizations
4   GROUP BY TYPE ORDER BY count(*);
```

Alerts

Sometimes, there is a business need to get notified when certain conditions are met (these can be positive as well as negative notifications).

For example, let's say you want to get notified by email about every deposit of more than USD 100 (we will create an alert for this specific example later on).

To view the existing alerts, simply click on **Alerts** in the upper left-hand side menu:

You will get to the **Alerts** list window, where you can see of all the available alerts, including their statuses.

Alerts only work on scheduled queries without parameters.

Alert statuses

Every time a scheduled query is executed, there is a check for an Alert status.

Currently, there are three status types for an Alert:

- **TRIGGERED**: This means that the condition you set for the alert met the conditions and the alert is on. Suppose you have a table that tracks logins to your API, and you set an alert on `distinct_user_logins_per_hour` > 100. If the query returns 105 logins per hour, for example, the alert will be triggered, and you will receive a notification through the channel you chose.
- **OK**: This means that the condition you set is either not met. This can happen both before the alert goes into the **TRIGGERED** state or after. In this example, we have it in the **TRIGGERED** state. Suppose the value of `distinct_user_logins_per_hour` changes to 70 – the alert will move from the **TRIGGERED** status to OK.
- **UNKNOWN**: This means that the query your alert is set for hasn't run yet. You can run the query manually to enforce the alert to check the conditions (not a must, since alerts work on scheduled queries. Eventually, it will run and check its status by itself).

Creating Alerts

In order to create a new alert, choose **Create | Alert** from the top menu:

You will be redirected to the search query phase, where you will have to pick the query you place the alert on:

 Currently, it is impossible to set an alert on parametrized queries.

Reminder: If you get the **mail server isn't configured** error (as shown in the following screenshot), you need to configure the mail server in Redash:

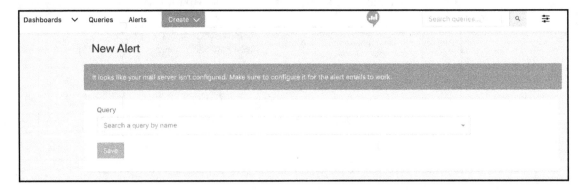

After you find the query you wish to place your alert on, you will get to the **Create Alert** screen itself:

Let's go over the fields:

- **Query**: The query you selected in the previous screen, that is, the one that the alert is relying on.
- **Name**: (In addition to the field, you can see it on top of the alert frame). This defaults to `$QUERY_NAME: $COLUMN $OPERATION $REFERENCE_VALUE`, but for your convenience, it's recommended to change it to something more meaningful for other users too.

- **Value Column**: The column that will be checked in order to trigger the alert.
- **Value**: The sample value of that column, only for your convenience (you can't edit this field – it's automatic).
- **Op**: An operator, such as greater than/less than/equals to.
- **Reference**: Your reference value (the actual value that the alert will be triggered on).
- **Rearm seconds**: The delay in seconds that Redash waits before *Rearming* (triggering) the alert.

- If you want the alert to be triggered only on status change, leave the **Rearm Seconds** value empty.

- If you want the alert to be triggered every time the query runs (for example, when you use it to monitor a critical component), set **Rearm Seconds** to a certain value, for example, 30 (which means that 30 seconds will pass from the time Redash detects if the alert should be triggered to the Notification action).

In our example in the preceding image, the alert will run on the query called **Events per hour**, which checks the number of events that have occurred during the last hour. Here is the query, for reference:

```
SELECT count(*) AS num_events
FROM EVENTS
WHERE extract(hour from created_at) = extract(hour from CURRENT_time) and
created_at>=current_date
```

The alert will be triggered when the num_events field value is **greater than 100**, and the alert will be sent **30** seconds after each query in run.

In addition to this, the name of the alert will be changed to something more meaningful like **High Number of Events Per Hour**.

After filling in all the fields, we will click on **Save** and choose the destinations and the recipients for the notifications:

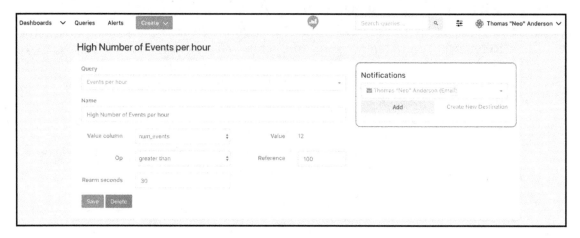

Clicking on **Save** again will finish the alert creation process.

It's a good practice to either run the query the alert is based on manually or wait for it to run by the scheduler, and get back to the **Alerts** list just to validate that the alert status is not **UNKNOWN** anymore:

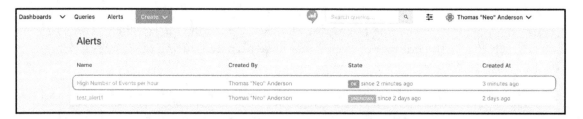

 Currently, there is no native option to trigger an alert based on more than one column.

 If you need to set an alert on multiple columns, you have to wrap it with a separate query (which is explained as follows).

For example, suppose you have a table called `critical_events`, and you're interested in three columns: `event_type`, `event_count`, and `event_owner`. You wish to trigger an alert when the **event_type** is `system_crash`, `event_count` is greater than `100`, and `event_owner` is **Neo Andersson**.

You have to create a `select` of the following form:

```
SELECT CASE
  WHEN event_type = 'system_crash'
  AND event_count > 100
  AND event_owner = 'Neo Andersson' THEN 1
  ELSE 0
  END AS trigger_cirical
FROM critical_events
```

What we did in the query is wrap all three columns into one condition (as in `trigger_critical` column), which returns either `1` (if the is condition met) or `0`. Now ,we can trigger the alert on the `trigger_critical` column for a value of `1`.

Alert destinations

Currently, five alert destinations are supported: Slack, Email, Mattermost, HipChat,ChatWork, and Webhook. (PagerDuty as an alert destination is currently in the development stage, and should be released before this book is published.)

 In order to add destinations, you need an Admin user, but after the destination is set, everyone can use it as an alert destination.

In order to view the available alert destinations, click on **Settings** and choose **Alert Destinations:**

When clicking on the **+ New Alert Destination** button, you will be redirected to a screen where you will define alert destinations:

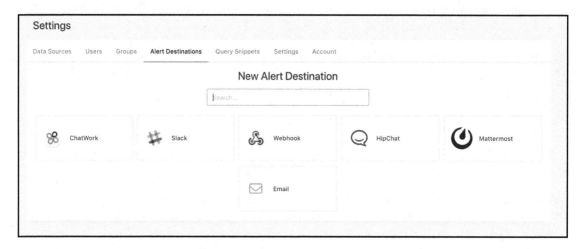

Start typing or click on one of the destination options.

When creating a destination, you will have to fill several fields such as destination name (to distinguish between several destinations), recipients (in case of email), WebHook URL (in case of **Slack / Mattermost / Webhook / HipChat**), Room ID and API Token in case of **ChatWork** and username/password when needed.

Summary

In this chapter, we covered the query editor, did an overview of its components, saw which operations we can do on queries, such as creating, listing, editing, cloning, archiving and scheduling, and saw what operations can be performed on query results, such as filtering, along with various format download options.

We saw what sharing options we have on queries, and covered the option of creating queries that accept parameters. Afterwards, we went over the query snippets and saw how can they make our query creation faster and easier.

In addition to this, we covered the alerting option provided by Redash so that we are able to stay updated on the most important metrics, even when we're not next to an open Redash tab in a browser.

6
Creating Visualizations

In the previous chapter, we managed to query our data sources and get raw results. Now, let's add some salt and pepper to make them easier to read.

Since Redash's primary audience is humans, and not machines, we can't ignore the fact that human eyes are able to receive and analyze information more easily through visuals and images rather than text and numbers.

Using visuals, it's much easier to spot complex trends, patterns, and anomalies in the data, as opposed to just staring at table results of it.

In this chapter, we will be covering the following topics:

- The benefits of visualizations
- An overview of visualization types
- Visualizations in action

The benefits of visualizations

Nowadays, people (and not necessarily analysts, or statisticians) get exposed to lots of data, whether it's business data (such as acquisitions, campaign revenue, or payments) or sensor data (such as average temperature, humidity, and barometric pressure).

In addition to the fact that the amount of data can be large, the data can contain *noise*, which obscures your insight. In most cases, the data comes unnormalized and has no proper reference points, which makes it harder to gain an insight into, especially for inexperienced analysts, or people who don't come from a statistical background.

These are the places where visualizing data comes in handy.

Consider the following example of daily active users (number of active users per day), as seen in the following table:

16/09/16	61
17/09/16	52
18/09/16	55
19/09/16	58
20/09/16	54
21/09/16	56
22/09/16	65
23/09/16	60
24/09/16	57
25/09/16	57
26/09/16	70
27/09/16	67
28/09/16	67
29/09/16	60
30/09/16	71

And in the following chart (the green arrows and red trend lines are drawn for convenience):

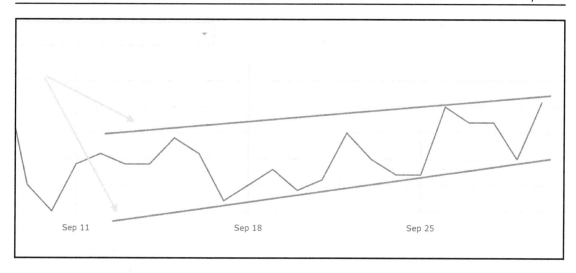

When looking at the chart, we can easily spot the positive trend (the increasing number of daily active users over time) with the naked eye, an insight we got in a matter of seconds, whereas looking at raw numbers will obviously require more time and effort to spot the same trend.

An overview of visualization types

Currently, Redash supports eleven visualization types (well, twelve, if you count the Table type, which is the default one you get. Table is also considered a visualization type), which we will discuss in the following subsections.

Boxplot

A boxplot is a visual representation of the **Five Number Summary**.

The Five Number Summary is a set of five statistical values that provide information about our dataset, and includes the following values:

- Minimum
- First quartile
- Median (second quartile)

- Third quartile
- Maximum

(The first quartile (Q_1) is defined as the middle number between the smallest number and the median of the dataset. The second quartile (Q_2) is the median of the data. The third quartile (Q_3) is the middle value between the median and the highest value of the dataset.)

The following is an example of a Boxplot in Redash:

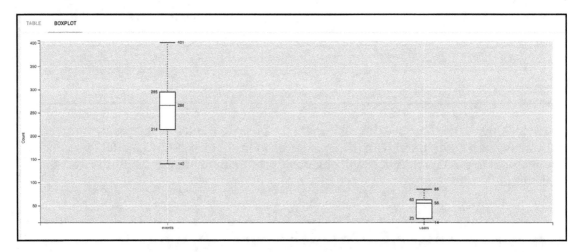

Boxplot in Redash

Chart

The chart type includes the following subtypes: line, bar, area chart, pie, and scatter.

It's a two dimensional visualization type, and is best used to represent time series data (daily/weekly values such as daily active users) and categorized values (for example, the number of sport clubs per city).

Pie charts can be used to show value distribution between different categories.

The following is an example of a line chart. This chart shows the number of user triggered events in Redash per hour in the past 3 days:

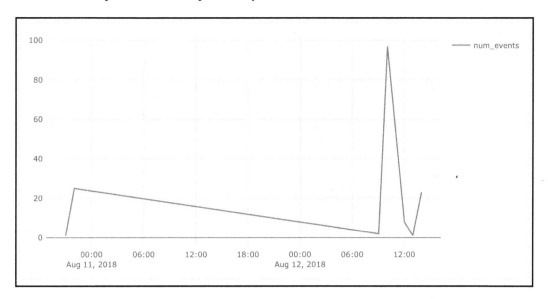

The following is an example of a bar chart, showing the number of queries per visualization type:

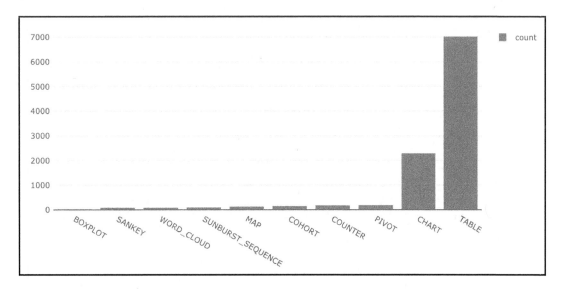

The following is an example of a pie chart, which uses the same query as the bar chart, but the visualization has been changed to pie:

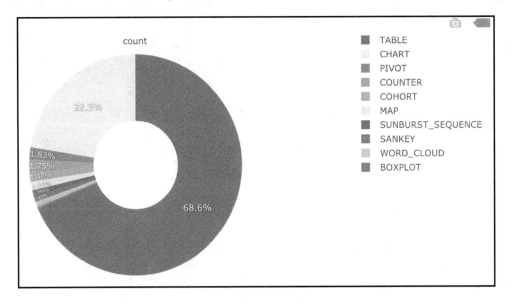

Pie chart visualization

The following is an example of a bar chart with stacking. This chart shows us the percentage of active Redash accounts, stacked by stage (source: `redash.io`):

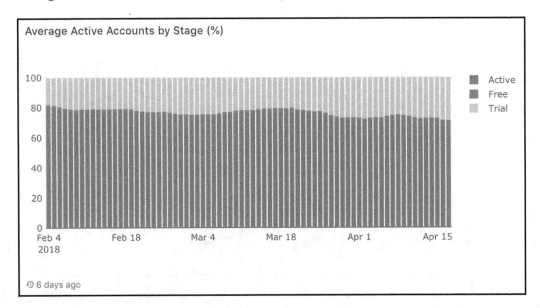

Map (Choropleth map)

A Choropleth map is a thematic map visualization, which allows you to mark areas (in Redash's case, it's **Countries**) according to specific values.

The countries are patterned according to the designated value (column), thus providing a convenient way to track distributions per country.

For example, the following Choropleth map shows the number of Redash users in different countries:

 Note that the minimal unit in a Choropleth is a *Country*. Currently, it's impossible to drill down into smaller areas.

Cohort

A cohort is a subset of objects that share some common characteristic. In data analytics (and more specifically, in our case) we will be referring to users who are grouped by shared characteristics. Usually, that characteristic is a certain type of *date*, for example, an acquisition date, and the first login date.

Users that were acquired on the same day are in the same cohort.

A **cohort analysis** allows us to compare the behavior and metrics of cohorts over time.

In the following cohort example, we can see the retention of users over 5 days (numbers from 1-5). Each *cohort* is determined by *Time*. Users from the first cohort are users that registered on the system on January 30th, and so on:

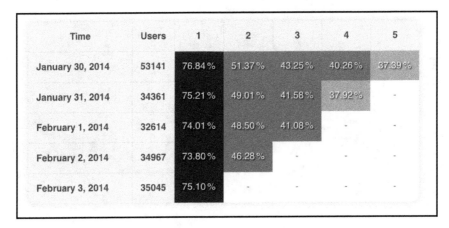

Time	Users	1	2	3	4	5
January 30, 2014	53141	76.84%	51.37%	43.25%	40.26%	37.39%
January 31, 2014	34361	75.21%	49.01%	41.58%	37.92%	-
February 1, 2014	32614	74.01%	48.50%	41.08%	-	-
February 2, 2014	34967	73.80%	46.28%	-	-	-
February 3, 2014	35045	75.10%	-	-	-	-

Counter

A counter is one of the simplest (yet effective) visualizations. In brief, it just displays a number, but sometimes, it's all you need to impress (for example, when showing total revenue).

The following is an example of a simple, yet impressive, counter:

$3,487,214
Total Revenue

Funnel

A funnel is a chart that visualizes a linear process that usually consists of several sequential steps.

The funnel consists of a top part, called the Head (or base), a bottom part, called the Neck, and in-between it, it has progressively decreasing values, in proportions amounting to 100 percent in total (the Head). Every step's size is determined by the series value as a percentage of the total of all values. It's also helpful to display, next to every step, the portion of the step itself as compared to the previous step (for example: step 3 is 20% of total, but 90% of step 2).

Although this chart is called a **funnel**, it differs from a physical funnel, because not everything that comes in (first step) comes out (last step). It is only called a funnel because of its shape.

The funnel chart is mostly used to visualize sales processes and reveal potentially problematic steps (areas that have the highest drop rate compared to the previous step).

In the following chart, I've chosen to draw a "Running Funnel", which shows the drop rates between several steps that people overcome before they actually go running:

Step towards Running	Number of Participants	% Max	% Previous
Bought Stop Watch	10,000	100.00%	100.00%
Bought Running Shoes	8,000	80.00%	80.00%
Bought Running Shorts	7,500	75.00%	93.75%
Bought Running Shirt	5,500	55.00%	73.33%
Started Running	3,000	30.00%	54.55%

Map (Markers map)

The Markers map differs from the choropleth map in the mapping option. Here, you're allowed to pinpoint any geolocation around the globe by providing its latitude and longitude.

This visualization is useful when you need to point out (mark) specific places.

In the following example, you can see the marks of **Napoli**, **Athens**, **Tel-Aviv**, and **Mumbai**:

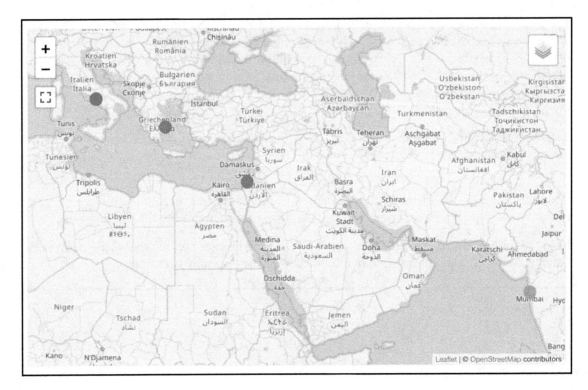

Pivot table

A pivot table is a table that summarizes data from another table (such as the result set) by applying an operation such as sorting, averaging, and summing to data in the first table, additionally including grouping and filtering the data by selectable columns.

It allows the user to view the data from various viewing points (pivots), hence the name. The user can change the filter/summary/group and the action of the "pivot" by dragging and dropping the desired columns.

The following pivot table below is based on a slightly modified visualization usage query

```
select distinct queries.name as "query_name", data_sources.name as
"datasource_name", visualizations.type as "visualization_type", count(*)
from visualizations join queries on visualizations.query_id = queries.id
join data_sources on data_sources.id= queries.data_source_id group by 1,2,3
order by 4 desc
```

and was made for presentation purposes only:

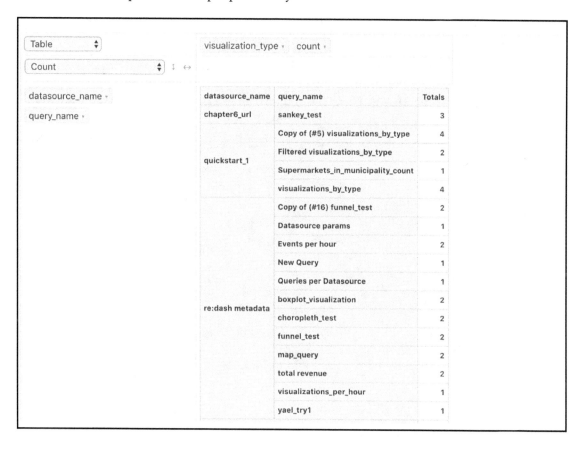

Sankey

The Sankey chart type is a type of a flow diagram in which the width of the connecting lines is shown proportionally to the flow quantity between the nodes that those lines connect to.

Sankey diagrams are typically used to visualize the flow of energy, material, or cost transfers between entities.

Sankey charts are specifically helpful in locating dominant contributions to an overall flow in the system.

Although it's not the primary use of Sankey, the following example illustrates use similar to the funnel chart. Here, we can see the flow of people who enter a building, go to the first floor, and enter offices **1a**, **1f**, and **1d**. In the connecting links, we can spot the amounts of those movements:

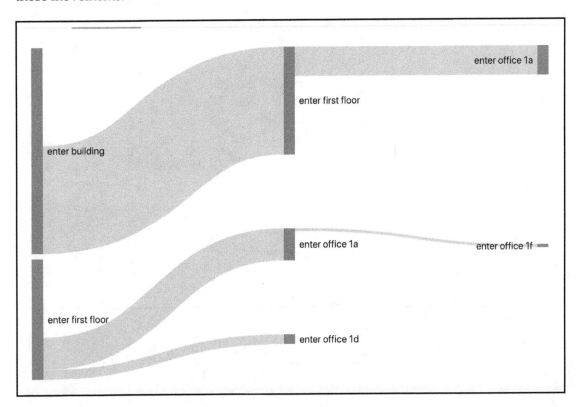

Sunburst sequence

The sunburst sequence chart can be referred to as a stacked pie chart. It is created by stacking the necessary amount of pie charts on top of each other. It is best used to represent hierarchical data where each and every level of the hierarchy is represented by one ring or circle within the innermost circle. A simple pie chart can represent a single dimension data, whereas stacking can represent multi-dimensional data.

The sunburst chart is most effective at showing how one ring is broken into its contributing pieces.

In the following chart, we used the same data of people who entered the building as in Sankey example. For example, we can easily spot that only 8.26% of the people who entered the building reached office **1a** (**Stage: 3**):

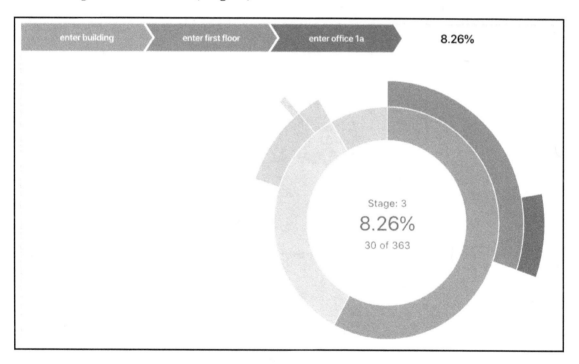

Word cloud

the word cloud is a visualisation that was initially used to display how frequently words appear in a given body of text by drawing each word with a size that is proportional to its frequency. Later, it was expanded to display words with a size proportional to any value provided, not necessarily the frequency of the word. For example, we could have a Country Name/Country Population word cloud.

In the following example, we can see the visualizations of the word cloud (all of the words are nearly the same size, since their usage is the same in the query results):

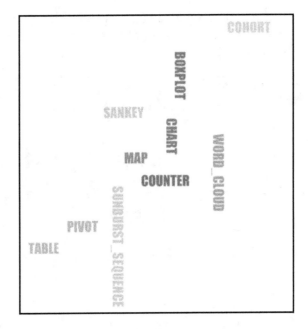

Table

Table is simply a tabular representation of the result set. Although it's the default option and everyone is familiar with it, we still mention it as a visualization type since it is one, and in addition, it can be customized according to your specific needs, making it worthwhile covering.

In the following table example, we can view the population of the United States in 1989:

_ID	TOTALPOP
CA	29,754,890
NY	17,990,402
TX	16,984,601
FL	12,686,644
PA	11,881,643
IL	11,427,576
OH	10,846,517
MI	9,295,297
NJ	7,730,188
NC	6,628,637
GA	6,478,216
VA	6,181,479
MA	6,016,425
IN	5,544,136
MO	5,110,648

< 1 2 3 4 >

Visualizations in action

In this section, we will review the process of creating and editing various visualizations that are available in Redash.

Visualizations are also referred to as *widgets*, especially in Redash code and documentation.

Creating and editing visualizations

In order to create a new visualization, the query must be **Saved**. If you didn't save the query in advance, when you start creating the visualization, the query will be saved automatically.

To create a new visualization, press the **+New Visualization** button:

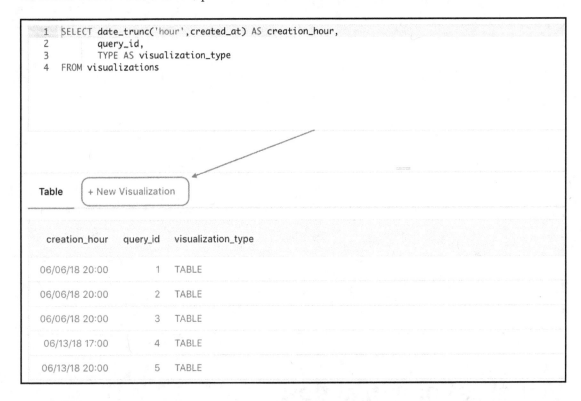

 Each query can have multiple visualizations!

After clicking on **+New Visualization**, you will enter the **Create Visualization** menu, which will be covered in detail for every chart type in the following sections:

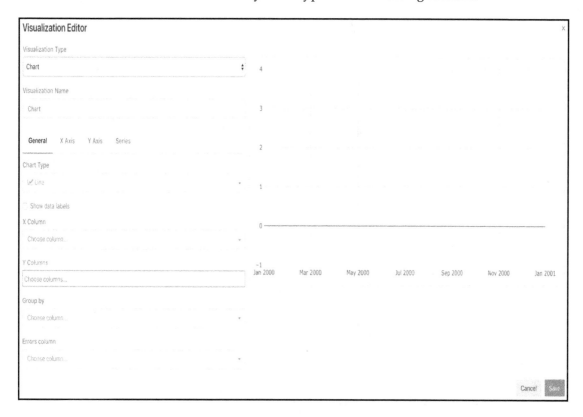

In order to edit a visualization, first, you must locate the query of that visualization and enter it (usually, it's enough to simply click the query link).

After finding your desired query and clicking on its link, you should get the following options:

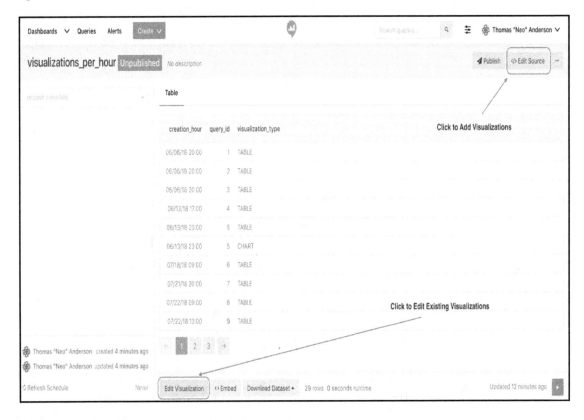

In order to add a new visualization, you first have to click on the **Edit Source** button (top right) to enter into edit query mode, which allows you to add new visualizations, like we saw previously.

In order to edit an existing visualization, click on the **Edit Visualization** button.

Going over Redash visualizations

Each Redash visualization type requires the data to come in its own *format*. In this section, we will go over all the visualizations that are available in Redash, and explain the process of adding each and every one of them.

All the explanations about visualization types are in the preceding *Visualization types overview* section.

Boxplot

In order to create a Boxplot, you must have only numeric columns in the query, since all of the parameters are calculated automatically.

In the following example, the query is as follows:

```
SELECT query_id, count(*) FROM visualizations GROUP BY query_id
```

This query returns the `query_id` and the `count` as numbers. Now, we will add the Boxplot to understand their distribution.

Choose **Boxplot** in **Visualization Type**, and add X/Y axis labels for your convenience.

Right after you select the visualization type, the Five Number Summary will be calculated automatically and drawn inside the visualization:

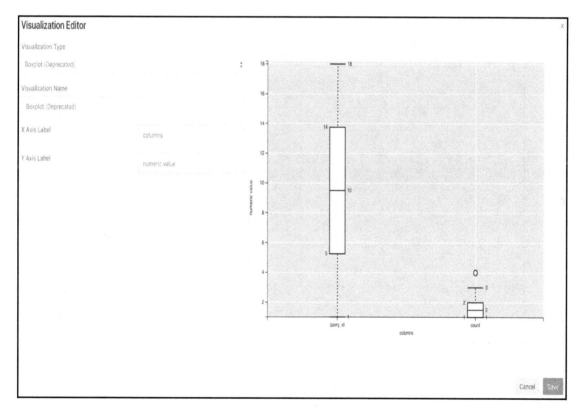

Illustration of Boxplot visualization type

Chart

Chart is one of the most customizable (and widely used) Redash visualization types. Select **Chart** in the **Visualization Type** field, and you will get to the chart menu. The chart menu has four tabs: **General**, **X Axis**, **Y Axis**, and **Series**. Let's start with the **General** tab:

The first thing you should select is the **Chart Type**. The available options are Line, Bar, Area, Pie, Scatter, Bubble and Box.

After selecting the suitable chart type, move on to selecting the X column and Y columns (note that you can select more than one column for the **Y Axis**).

Toggle the **Show Data Labels** checkbox if you want to display the value of each datapoint on the point itself inside the chart.

Group by column is used to define categories for the chart. For example, you have a line chart that represents daily active users per country; selecting the country as group by column will create a separate line for each country.

When **Show Legend** is unchecked, this disables the Legend display on the top right corner.

When `Stacking` is selected, it stacks values one on top of the other (for different categories).

Considering **Normalize Values to Percentages**, as the name suggests, it normalizes the values to 100%.

After you are finished with the **General** tab, we can move on to customizing the **X Axis**:

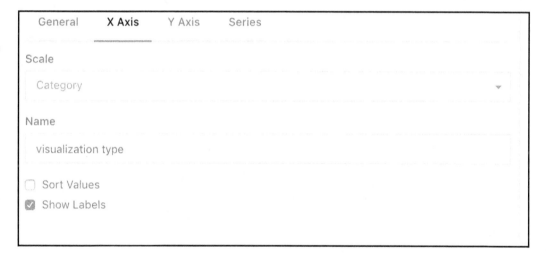

The **Scale** is the most important one. Here, you define whether your **X Axis** is of datetime, Linear, Logarithmic, or Category scale.

Name is the **X Axis'** name.

Regarding **Sort values**, in come cases (not when using datetime), you want to sort the **X Axis** values (when the **Scale** is **Category**). If so, toggle this checkbox.

Show Labels shows the labels of values along the **X Axis**.

The following is a visual of the **Y Axis** tab:

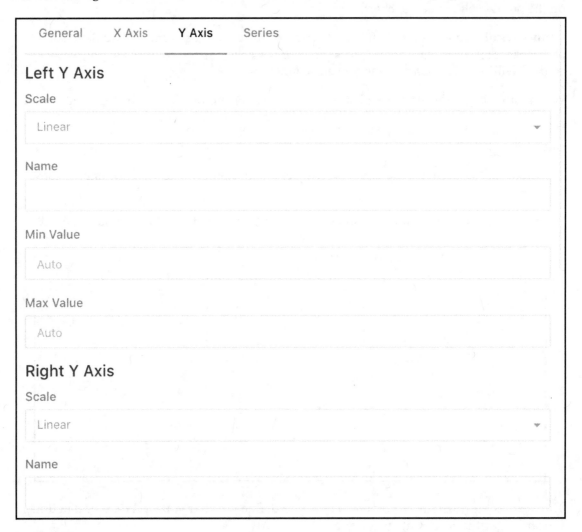

As seen from the screen shot, you can have two Y axes.

In addition to scale (which you also had in **X Axis**), this allows you to set the min/max value (in case you're not interested in automatic discovery based on your data).

In the **Series** tab, you can control the colors and labels of your series (especially when you have more than one).

Map (Choropleth)

After selecting Map (Choropleth) in the **Visualization Type**, you will get three Control tabs to fully customize it: **General**, **Colors**, and **Bounds**.

In the **General Tab**, you can select the country column (as well as the format of its values, for example, a 2 or 3 letter ISO).

Here, you can select the **Value** column (according to which the countries will be painted), control the formatting of the values, and customize tooltips (when hovering over country) and popups (when clicking on country) by simple DSL:

In the **Colors** tab, you get to control the way countries are painted. Here, you can set Min / Max colour for painting options, and use clustered mode for adjacent countries to paint:

In the **Bounds** tab, you can set rectangular boundaries for a region of interest on the map, the boundaries are in format of decimal lat / lon (for example 47.3769,8.5417). The boundaries are used to "pre-zoom" on the desired area, for convenience:

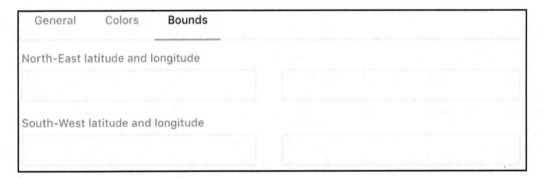

Cohort

After selecting Cohort in **Visualization Type**, you get to control two tabs: **Columns** and **Options**.

In the **Columns** tab, you select the **Bucket** column (data-based), the **Stage** column (defines the different stages for your cohort), the **Bucket Population Size** (column that has the total size of the initial Bucket), and the **Stage Value** (the column that has the value for cohort stages):

In the **Options** tab, you can select **Time Interval** (**Daily/Monthly** cohorts) and an option to fill the empty values with zeros if need be:

Counter

After selecting **Counter** as the **Visualization Type**, you will be surprised that despite being a very simple type, it allows a lot of flexibility when it comes to customizing it.

In the **General** tab, you can select the **Counter** column, and in case the value is part of some "target" value (for example, **Daily Revenue** as **Counter**, or **Desired Monthly Revenue** as **Target**) you need to select the "target" column also.

In case the "target" is selected, the counter visualization will appear in the form of **Counter_Value (Target_Value)**

If you check **Count Rows**, the counter will simply display the row count instead of the value in the **Counter** column:

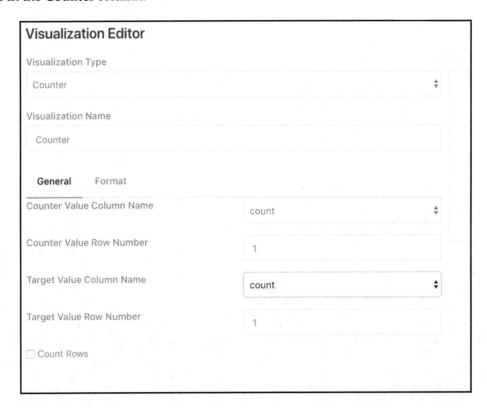

In the **Format** tab, you get to control the value formatting, such as **Formatting Decimal Place**, **Formatting Decimal Character**, **Formatting Thousands Separator**, and **Formatting String Prefix**:

Funnel

After picking Funnel in the **Visualization Type**, you can select the **Step** column name (which defines the steps within the funnel), which is where you can set a custom display name for that column.

You can select the **Funnel Value Column Name** (which holds the value for each step), and set a custom name for that column as well.

All the other options are calculated by Redash (such as the percentage of total and percentage of previous step):

Map (Markers)

Select **Map (Markers)** in **Visualization Type**.

You will have three tabs to customize: **General**, **Groups**, and **Map Settings**.

In the **General** tab, you can select the **Latitude Column Name** and **Longitude Column Name**, as well as the **Group By** column, which is used for series (Groups):

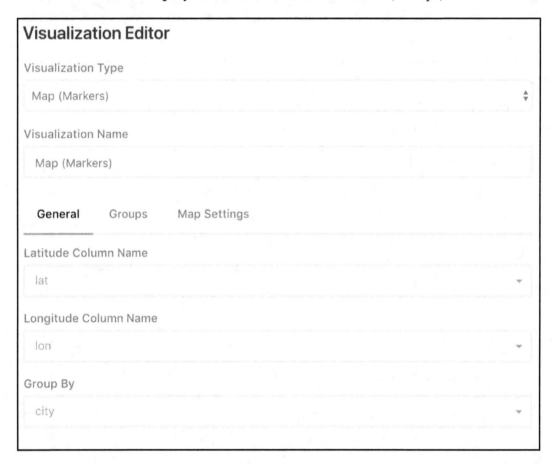

In the **Groups** tab, you get to pick the color for each group (in case the random default colors were not good enough):

In the **Map Settings** tab, you can change the visual representation of the Map itself. For example, you can select **Topographical Map** instead of **Street Map**.
**Cluster Markers checkbox: allows us to combine markers that are close one to another into "clusters", to optimize their display on the map.
instead of seeing multiple markers on the same point, you will see a bigger mark (cluster) with a number in it (number represents the number of single marks within the cluster), as you zoom in - you will see fewer marks within the cluster, and more individual markers.**

Pivot Table

In the **Pivot Table** visualization type, you create the Pivot options in the same manner as in Excel by selecting the grouping action and then playing with the columns/rows.

In case you don't want to provide the end user with flexibility of changing pivot values, you can check the **Hide Pivot Controls** checkbox:

Sankey

After selecting **Sankey** as the **Visualization Type**, Redash doesn't let you to customize anything, but rather displays help of how the values of your query should be arranged.

Note that here, it is talking about rows:

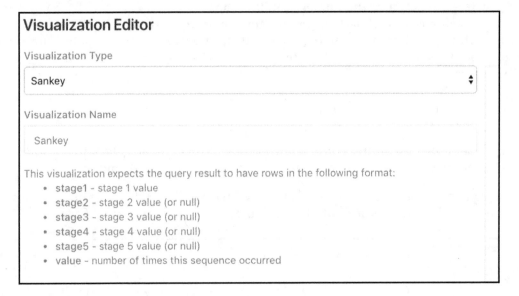

Sunburst sequence

Similar to **Sankey**, for the **Sunburst Sequence**, you just need to provide query results aligned with the following description:

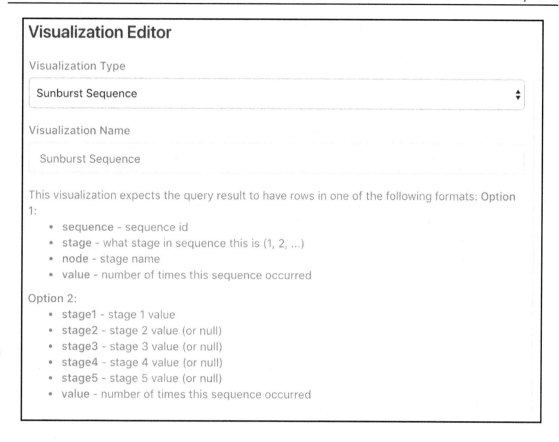

Table

Table is the default visualization, and hence most of the time, you won't need to select it in **Visualization Type**.

For the **Table Visualization Type**, you have two tabs to customize: **Columns** and **Grid**.

In the **Columns** tab, Redash allows you to control the column's layout.

When the **Use for Search** checkbox is checked, you can search values on that column.

Display as is used for value formatting options.

Allow HTML content (for string types) allows you to embed and parse HTML content as part of the value.

Highlight links (for string types) speaks for itself :

The **Grid** tab allows you to control the maximum number of records per display page

Word Cloud

Select Word Cloud as the **Visualization Type**.

In **Word Cloud Visualization Type**, you must select the column which holds the names – Redash does the rest:

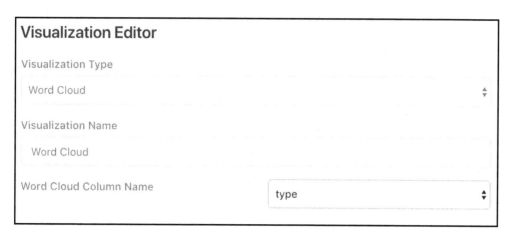

Special actions on visualizations

Several widgets (for example, Chart Visualizations) have special menus on them (hover over them with the mouse on the top right corner of the widget itself, and you will see the menu).

It contains the following options (from left to right):

- Download plot as PNG
- Zoom (by selection)
- Pan
- Zoom in
- Zoom out

- Autoscale
- Reset Axis to initial value
- Toggle spike lines (helps to see the values)
- Show closest data on hover
- Compare data on hover

The most useful one is the first one (marked with an arrow), which is Download plot as PNG:

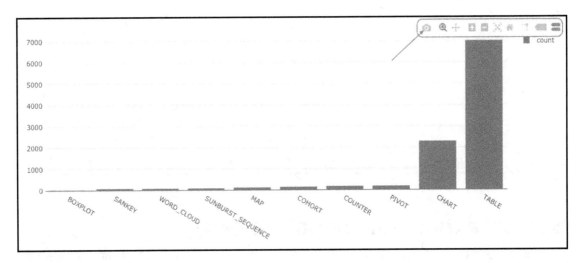

Sometimes, there is a need to embed a visualization (widget) in an external website, and still keep it refreshed when the data source changes. Redash allows you to do just that.

On the bottom left menu, click on the <>**Embed** button. A dialog will pop up, with the visualization already appended inside an *iframe*, which can be embedded in any web page you wish (you just need to copy the popped up code, and paste it into your destination website):

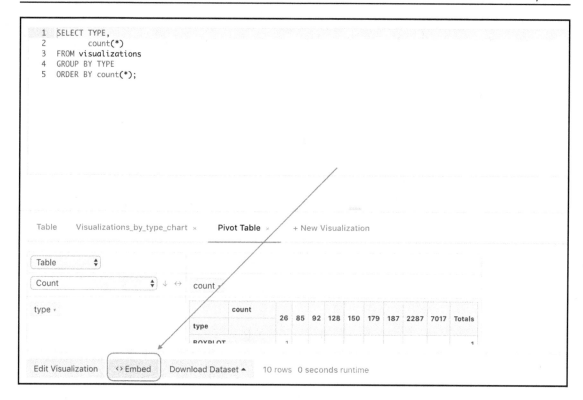

```
1  SELECT TYPE,
2         count(*)
3  FROM visualizations
4  GROUP BY TYPE
5  ORDER BY count(*);
```

Table   Visualizations_by_type_chart ×   **Pivot Table** ×   + New Visualization

Table ⬍

Count ⬍ ↓ ↔ count ⬍

type ⬍		count									
	type		26	85	92	128	150	179	187	2287	7017	Totals
	BOXPLOT		1									1

Edit Visualization   <> Embed   Download Dataset ▲   10 rows 0 seconds runtime

Summary

In this chapter, we have learned what the immediate benefits of adding visualizations to your data are, went over supported visualization types in Redash, and seen when to use each and every type.

We've had hands-on experience in creating and editing the supported Visualization types, as well as learning special actions that we can perform on the visualizations, such as export as image, and embed as iframe.

In the next chapter, we will cover advanced tips for creating better dashboards for your management and business departments, allowing them to rapidly find answers to their business questions.

Dashboards and Practical Tips

7

After reviewing all of the possible visualization options in Redash, it's about time that we learn how to wrap and present it to the relevant entities.

Dashboards are usually the culmination of an analytical process, so it's a real opportunity to enhance the effect of these insights, thus making interpretation of the results nice and easy.

A single visualization can help you spot a trend, while a well planned dashboard can give you multiple trends for numerous metrics, more of a 360° view of the problem, and truly back a business decision (for example, expanding to a vertical or completely abandoning a moderately profitable campaign).

On the other hand, lack of planning in the presentational layer might cause the viewers of the dashboard to miss the point, or get only a partial picture of the topic presented.

In this chapter, we will be covering the following topics:

- Dashboard how-tos
- Dashboard guidelines
- Tips and tricks

Dashboard how-tos

In `Chapter 3`, *Creating and Visualizing your First Query*, we already saw in brief how to create a basic dashboard, and in this section, we'll take a deeper dive into it.

Creating/editing dashboards

Creating dashboards was already covered in `Chapter 3`, *Creating and Visualizing your First Query*.

Clicking on **Dashboards** in the top-left corner will bring you to the dashboards screen, where you can see your already created dashboards.

To edit a dashboard, simply find the dashboard in the **Dashboards** screen or use the search box. Click on it to go to the dashboard itself and, from within the dashboard's top-right menu, select **Edit**. You will enter the **Edit Dashboard** screen, where you will be able to add/modify/remove widgets and rename the dashboard.

- Edit controls:
    - When in **Edit Mode**, clicking on the **X** (top-right corner of each widget) will remove the widget from the dashboard
    - The widgets can be moved around the dashboard layout if you click and hold while moving
    - The widgets are resizable; just point the mouse at any edge of the widget, and you should see a resize control:

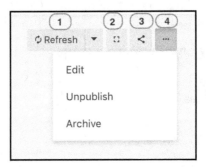

Let's quickly review the **Dashboards** menu:

- **Refresh intervals for the dashboard**: Controls how often the dashboard's underlying queries will be refreshed.
- **Full Screen option**: Toggles full screen mode for the dashboard.
- **Share option**: Options for sharing the dashboard.

- **Actions submenu (contains Edit/Unpublish/Archive)**: **Unpublish** will not be available if the dashboard is not published yet (obviously). **Archive** is instead of **Delete**, exactly as in queries; all it means is that direct links to the dashboard will continue to work, while the dashboard won't be available in searches, nor will the dashboards list.

Dashboard query filters, hashtags, and favorite dashboards

To provide more control and convenience to the user, Redash offers the ability to apply filters on all of the dashboard queries at once, and group dashboards based on user-defined tags (**#hashtags**).

In addition, you can mark dashboard as favorite (exactly as you did in queries) for quicker access to your favorite dashboards.

When in edit **Dashboard** mode, you can see the following controls, as shown in the following screenshot:

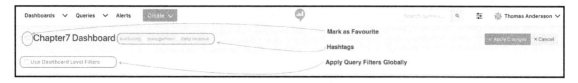

Favorites, hashtags and global filter controls

Dashboard-level filters

If we have queries with filters (refer to `Chapter 5`, *Writing and Executing Queries*), we would like to apply those filters on the dashboard level.

To do so, in **Edit Dashboard** mode, simply check the **Use Dashboard Level Filters** checkbox (and don't forget to click **Apply Changes** on the right!).

From now on, the filters will be applied to all queries on this dashboard.

Dashboard hashtags

There is an option to **Group Dashboards** by using `#hashtags` in the dashboard name.

This comes in handy when you have a lot of themed dashboards, for example, several dashboards for the `#IT department` containing `#monitoring` of `#virtual-machines`, `#switch-metrics`, and `#open` `#incidents`, or for `#marketing` and `#sales` `departments`, you could have `#client-revenue`, `#active-campaigns`, and `#open-leads` dashboards.

To add a `#hashtag` to a dashboard, click on the **Edit** icon on the right of the dashboard's name, and simply append a new hashtag to existing ones (while in **Edit Dashboard** mode):

After saving your dashboard, you will find the `#hashtags` and the related dashboards on the **Dashboards** screen:

The #hashtags on the right (under the search box and **Favorites**) are clickable. Clicking on them will filter the dashboards in the list to contain only the dashboards that have the clicked #hashtag in their name.

Favorite Dashboards

Everyone has their own favorites, and that's also true for dashboards.

Mark dashboards as favorites by checking the star next to the dashboard's name, and your favorite dashboards will be easily accessible through the Favorites menu:

Keeping naming conventions in hashtags is highly recommended.

Sharing dashboards

If you wish to embed a dashboard in some external (external to Redash, but still within your company) web page, you can use the URL from the **Full Screen** mode of the dashboard.

To obtain it, click on **Full Screen** mode in the **Dashboard** menu and copy the URL.

The URL should be of the following structure (note the `?fullscreen` suffix): `http://your_redash_host.com/dashboard/your_dashboard?fullscreen`.

 The embedding method is good for web pages within your company, since it will still require users to be logged in to Redash!

If you wish to share the dashboard with someone external to your company (without having them log in to Redash), click on the **Share** option in the **Dashboard** menu. You will see a pop-up dialog, where you have to check the **Allow public access (using a secret URL)** checkbox.

After checking it, you will see the shareable URL underneath, as in the following screenshot:

You can now copy the URL and share it with your external users.

The shared dashboard doesn't contain any controls or buttons, only the widgets in the exact same layout as your dashboard.

Dashboard guidelines

While individual queries and visualizations can be created for the analysts themselves, dashboards are usually created for a specific client. That client can be the head of the Marketing department, VP Sales, your CEO, or your external partners.

Every single one of them has different demands and points of interest, and it's your goal to understand them.

Before starting to build the dashboard, ask yourself two questions:

- Who am I building the dashboard for?
- What am I going to show on this dashboard?

The first question is important, since here you are going to restrict yourself to specific visualization types.

For example, you probably won't be using the sunburst sequence when creating a monitoring dashboard for your Operations team.

Although highly subjective, **Sankey** and **Sunburst Sequence** visualizations are more marketing-oriented visualizations. They can suit sales dashboards or other presentational dashboards very well, but for the IT/Operations department, you have to present highly practical, possibly minimalistic dashboards. The Operations team needs to be able to quickly spot anomalies and decide whether the current state is normal or we're about to enter a crisis. The visualizations should contain trend charts, which allow you to compare performance between different servers and different environments.

Another example is that you won't be using a boxplot when presenting a dashboard to the sales or marketing department. They don't need to care about the statistical distribution of your values; they need to see a client's geodistribution (maps are excellent candidates) to understand where across the globe our product is popular, and they need to see clear revenue values. For summary revenues, it's not discouraged to have a single-value visualization.

Stacked bar charts are used to see revenue per partner, since the stacking will help us spot the most contributive partner, as well as the partner that should get a little motivational talk.

The second question should target the queries that you have to write. Queries are the exact questions that you seek answers for.

You can ask a helper question, such as *what are the KPIs I'm expected to expose?*

These will determine which data sources you are going to connect to and what level of data granularity is expected. For example, the Operations department might require hourly or even minute-to-minute data, while the CEO will require daily reports.

Also, now's the time to plan the themes of your dashboard. You don't always want to mix different topics in the same dashboard (unless you're playing with Redash for yourself, or trying to impress your team leader). For the Accounting department, for example, you might want to maintain two dashboards, **Expenses** and **Income**. Both can be split into departments, thus allowing you to spot the most profitable department and the one that spends the most.

As you already know, you can create several visualizations for each query, and that's an excellent reason to experiment; don't fear creating dashboards for the same queries by using different visualizations. Treat it as the A/B testing of your dashboards to spot the one that really makes the difference.

Since Redash it very intuitive and simple to use, you can be the one that creates the queries and visualizations, and every end client (such as VP Marketing/VP Sales) can create and customize their own personal dashboard according to their style preferences.

The suggestions presented here are not set in stone, and your own discoveries through experiments might reveal the opposite of what was suggested here (for example, a Sales department that prefers only plain numbers, or an IT department that fell in love with Sankey diagrams).

Tips and tricks

When you want to quickly test whether a certain visualization is suitable for your needs, but you don't have the time to create the long and complex query that will provide you the necessary results in the format the visualization expects, you can simply mock the result set and do your quick and dirty test.

Here is an example, Suppose I want to test the funnel visualization. I know that the funnel expects a column for the **Funnel Steps** and another column for the **Funnel Step Value**. I select the internal Redash data source, called Redash metadata (no worries, we don't need anything from the data in the data source itself), and execute the following query:

```
SELECT 'Bought Stop Watch' AS fun_step,
       10000 AS
VALUES
UNION
  (SELECT 'Bought Running Shoes' AS fun_step,
          8000 AS
   VALUES)
UNION
  (SELECT 'Bought Running Shorts' AS fun_step,
          7500 AS
   VALUES)
UNION
  (SELECT 'Bought Running Shirt' AS fun_step,
          5500 AS
   VALUES)
UNION
  (SELECT 'Started Running' AS fun_step,
          3000 AS
   VALUES)
```

Please note that this is just a mockup query; it doesn't use any tables, and it just creates five records with static values:

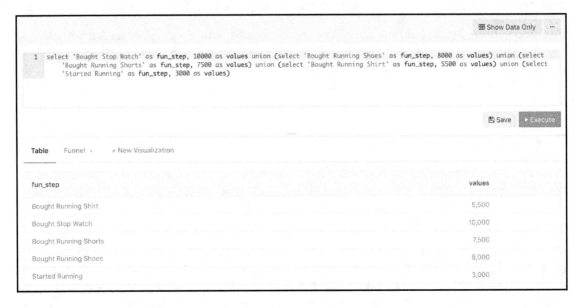

However, it's more than enough to create and test our **Funnel** visualization:

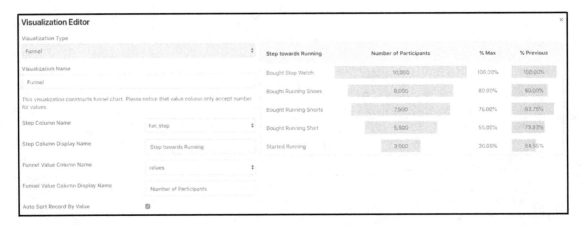

Funnel visualization

Now, we can get the feel of the visualization we want to test, as well as the ability to place it in a dashboard, and see if it helps our insights.

Here is another example of a mockup query for Map (Markers). The query is simply hardcoded with the latitude/longitude of four randomly selected cities:

```
SELECT 32.0853 AS lat,
  34.7818 AS lon,
  'Tel Aviv' AS city
UNION
  (SELECT 37.9838 AS lat,
  23.7275 AS lon,
  'Athens' AS city)
UNION
  (SELECT 40.8518 AS lat,
  14.2681 AS lon,
  'Napoli' AS city)
UNION
  (SELECT 19.0760 AS lat,
  72.8777 AS lon,
  'Mumbay' AS city)
```

This is the dataset that you should get when executing the query:

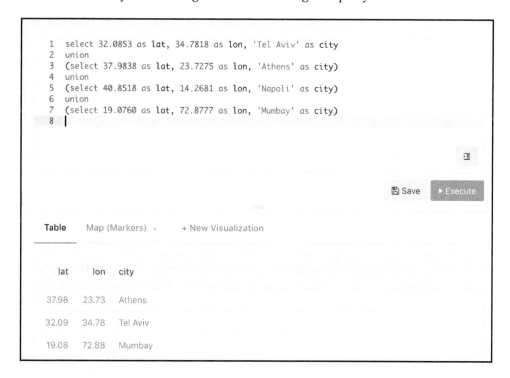

And this is what the map visualization will look like, based on the preceding dataset:

Map Visualization on the dataset

Don't be afraid to experiment with your own mockups. Redash is a very powerful (yet simple) tool that allows you to move faster when designing and building dashboards.

A very useful resource for up-to-date tips and tricks from the Redash community can be found here: `https://discuss.redash.io/c/tips-tricks-query-examples`.

Summary

In this chapter, we went over actions that can be performed with **Dashboards**, reviewed **Edit Dashboard** mode, explored the ability to group dashboards by hashtags, and explored filtering all of the visualizations inside a dashboard using dashboard-level filters.

Finally, we went through some generic guidelines on how to design and create dashboards, as well as some mocking tips that can help you experiment faster.

In the next chapter, we will be talking about options for extending Redash.

8
Customizing Redash

While Redash provides a fistful of features and available data `sources/visualizations/dashboard layouts/alerts` out of the box, it's not always enough to fulfill the needs of all of your users.

Data sources are very dynamic, and it won't be a mistake to note that you can definitely expect at least one/two totally new and not widely known data sources to become mainstream per year.

The same goes for alert destinations. For example, one day an email alert is enough, but as your company expands in new directions, you want Slack or Mattermost, or maybe Skype integration.

Your department manager is happy with the current dashboard layout and visualization type, but tomorrow you get a bigger screen to display your dashboards on, and all of a sudden you need a flower-shaped chart visualization.

If you use one of the closed source legacy dashboarding tools, you might have to wait until your newly requested features make their way to the product manager of that tool, and then probably for several development/QA cycles until it propagates to public release.

At this point, one of the main benefits of Redash is the fact that Redash is open source, and you can tailor it to meet your own needs by yourself.

In the following sections, we will cover options regarding extending Redash beyond the basics that came with it out of the box.

In this chapter, we will be covering the following topics:

- Redash API
- API calls overview
- API usage examples
- Extending Redash code

Redash API

Redash exposes the REST API for most of its features, allowing a lot of possibilities so that you can customize and extend it to meet your own needs.

As part of this chapter, we will cover the exposed API methods, as well as some real world ideas for their use.

API authentication

All of the API calls in Redash support authentication with an API key. Redash has two types of API keys:

- **User API Key**: This has the same permissions as the user who owns it, and can be found on the user profile page. Click on **Users** in the top-right corner and choose **Edit Profile**:

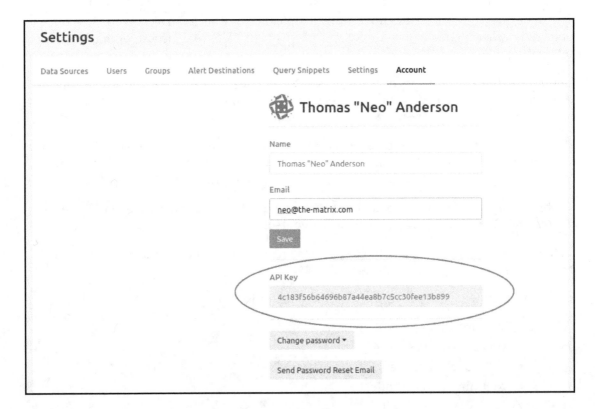

- **Query API Key**: This only has access to the query and its results, and can be found on the query page. Click on the **query menu** (1) and choose **Show API Key** (2):

After clicking on **Show API Key**, you should get the following screen where you can see the key, and an example of how to use it in an actual API call (you can actually test that by copying the URL and pasting it into your browser window):

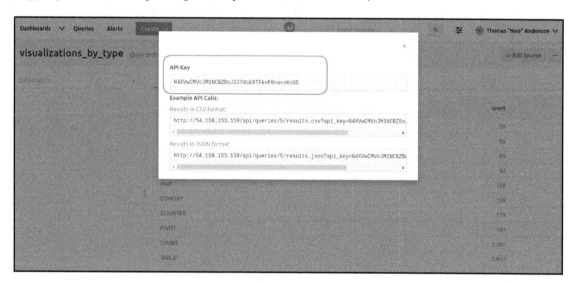

 Whenever possible, we recommend using a query API Key.

API calls overview

The API allows HTTP GET, HTTP POST, and HTTP DELETE calls.

GET is used to retrieve data (JSON format), POST is used to add/update data (for example, adding a new alert subscriber), and DELETE is used to delete data (for example, deleting a user).

All of the GET API calls can be easily tested with a browser (just paste the full URL and you will receive the JSON output on your screen).

For POST and DELETE, you will have to use **cURL**, write your own code, or use the tools available for working with REST API calls.

The paths presented here are **relative** to the root path of Redash.

For example, if my Redash is located at myredash.mydomain.com and I'm interested in the API located at /api/alerts, then the full URL will be http://myewdash.mydomain.com/api/alerts.

Let's make an example API call to retrieve the query details of the query with id=7034. I will be using curl the command; the api_key should be obtained. In this example, I'm using the Redash located at demo.redash.io. It is publicly accessible, so you will be able to see the results by executing the following command on your own computer, too:

cURL: http://demo.redash.io/api/queries/7034?api_key=
PVZnoWp8dzpOc39nqrltmhShKgC712k2I67M0zWR.

The results are returned as JSON:

```
{
 "latest_query_data_id": 4858254,
 "schedule": null,
 "is_archived": false,
 "updated_at": "2018-06-19T13:59:14.086188+00:00",
 "user": {
 "auth_type": "external",
 "created_at": "2018-03-25T22:47:14.445079+00:00",
 "name": "Alexander Leibzon",
 "gravatar_url":
"https://www.gravatar.com/avatar/ec8c207871ac01f536886d27d80d215d?s=40",
 "updated_at": "2018-03-25T22:47:14.445079+00:00",
 "id": 31659,
 "groups": [2],
 "email": "alexander.leibzon@gmail.com"
```

```
        },
        "query": "select count(*) from queries;",
        "is_draft": true,
        "id": 7034,
        "description": null,
        "can_edit": false,
        "name": "inner_test1",
        "created_at": "2018-06-11T14:44:52.260418+00:00",
        "last_modified_by": {
        "auth_type": "external",
        "created_at": "2018-03-25T22:47:14.445079+00:00",
        "name": "Alexander Leibzon",
        "gravatar_url":
"https://www.gravatar.com/avatar/ec8c207871ac01f536886d27d80d215d?s=40",
        "updated_at": "2018-03-25T22:47:14.445079+00:00",
        "id": 31659,
        "groups": [2],
        "email": "alexander@leibzon.com"
        },
        "version": 1,
        "query_hash": "8edff20893be2fe567819947d9735177",
        "visualizations": [{
        "description": "",
        "created_at": "2018-06-11T14:44:52.260418+00:00",
        "updated_at": "2018-06-11T14:44:52.260418+00:00",
        "id": 10603,
        "type": "TABLE",
        "options": {},
        "name": "Table"
        }],
        "api_key": "PVZnoWp8dzpOc39nqrltmhShKgC712k2I67M0zWR",
        "options": {
        "parameters": []
        },
        "data_source_id": 2
        }
```

Note that, in case you forget about the authentication and try to make a call without api_key, you will get the following error:

```
curl http://demo.redash.io/api/queries/7034
{
"message": "Couldn't find resource. Please login and try again."
}
```

This is an overview of all the possible API calls supported in Redash.

You can find them all in the `api.py` file (located in `$REDASH_DIR/redash/handlers/api.py`).

In this secion, the API calls are grouped by themes, with explanations about every group of API calls:

- **Alert**: related API calls allow us to **View/Add/Modify** alerts, as well as add and remove subscribers to/from a certain alert:
  - `/api/alerts`
  - `/api/alerts/<alert_id>`
  - `/api/alerts/<alert_id>/subscriptions`
  - `/api/alerts/<alert_id>/subscriptions/<subscriber_id>`
- **Dashboard**: related API calls allow us to **View/Add/Modify** dashboards, see a recent dashboard, list public ones, and share them (allowing anonymous access to the dashboard):
  - `/api/dashboards`
  - `/api/dashboards/recent`
  - `/api/dashboards/<dashboard_slug>`
  - `/api/dashboards/public/<token>`
  - `/api/dashboards/<dashboard_id>/share`
- **Data source**: related API calls allow us to view, modify, add, and delete data sources, as well as test the connection, get the schema (for a specific data source), and pause a specific data source:
  - `/api/data_sources`
  - `/api/data_sources/types`
  - `/api/data_sources/<data_source_id>/schema`
  - `/api/data_sources/<data_source_id>/pause`
  - `/api/data_sources/<data_source_id>/test`
  - `/api/data_sources/<data_source_id>`
- Group-related API calls allow us to view, modify, add, and delete groups, manage users as members of groups, and manage data sources as members of groups:
  - `/api/groups`
  - `/api/groups/<group_id>`
  - `/api/groups/<group_id>/members`
  - `/api/groups/<group_id>/members/<user_id>`
  - `/api/groups/<group_id>/data_sources`

- `/api/groups/<group_id>/data_sources/<data_source_id>`
- The following is an API call that shows all the recent events that have occurred in the system:
  - `/api/events`
- **Query**: related API calls allow us to view, modify, add, and delete queries, as well as view recent/user-only queries, search queries, trigger query results and refresh them, fork a query, and download its dataset as a `.csv/.json` file:
  - `/api/queries`
  - `/api/queries/search`
  - `/api/queries/recent`
  - `/api/queries/my`
  - `/api/queries/<query_id>/refresh`
  - `/api/queries/<query_id>`
  - `/api/queries/<query_id>/fork`
  - `/api/queries/<query_id>/results.<filetype>`
  - `/api/queries/<query_id>/results/<query_result_id>.<filetype>`
- **ACL (Access Control List)**: related API calls and API calls related to security allow us to view and modify the access policy on a certain object (a query, widget, dashboard, and so on):
  - `/api/<object_type>/<object_id>/acl`
  - `/api/<object_type>/<object_id>/acl/<access_type>`
- **Query results**: related API calls allow us to view and download query results:
  - `/api/query_results`
  - `/api/query_results/<query_result_id>.<filetype>`
  - `/api/query_results/<query_result_id>`
- **Job**: related API calls allow us to retrieve information about a running query job or cancel a running query job:
  - `/api/jobs/<job_id>`
- **Users**: related API calls allow us to view, modify, add, and disable users, invite users by email, and reset a user's password:
  - `/api/users`
  - `/api/users/<user_id>`
  - `/api/users/<user_id>/invite`

- `/api/users/<user_id>/reset_password`
- `/api/users/<user_id>/disable`
- **Visualization**: related API calls allow us to view, modify, add, and delete visualizations:
  - `/api/visualizations`
  - `/api/visualizations/<visualization_id>`
- **Widgets**: related API calls allow us to view, modify, add, and delete widgets:
  - `/api/widgets`
  - `/api/widgets/<int:widget_id>`
- **Alert destinations**: related API calls allow us to view, modify, add, and delete Alert type destinations:
  - `/api/destinations`
  - `/api/destinations/types`
  - `/api/destinations/<destination_id>`
  - Query snippets related to API calls allow us to view, modify, add, and delete query snippets:
  - `/api/query_snippets`
  - `/api/query_snippets/<snippet_id>`
  - API- related global Redash settings allow us to **View/Add/Modify** global settings (for example, `date_format`, Google app domains, and so on):
  - `/api/settings/organization`

API usage examples

The use cases for an API can be (but are definitely not limited to) any of the following:

- You want to use Redash query results but visualize them with your own proprietary charts. For example, you have an existing dashboard with your own visualizations and styles, and you only want to use the data from Redash. The query results export was made exactly for that.
- You can trigger a query refresh by using an external scheduler.
- Backup and restore (for example, export all of your queries to files).

- Add/remove users as a post action from your other products. For example, new user logins to your system can trigger automatic user creation in Redash, and the same is true for user deletion.
- Auditing and monitoring can be used to see how many jobs are running at the current time in the system, report query freshness, calculate the most active users, and much more. Of course, the API is not limited to these uses, and every other use case is strongly encouraged!

Extending Redash code

In case just using the API doesn't suit all your needs, you are more than welcome to get into the code itself, and if the feature is useful for other people/organizations, it's more than encouraged to create a **Pull Request** and become a Redash Contributor.

 Familiarity with `Docker/Node.js/Python/Angular.js/React.js/Git` is highly recommended.

Installing Redash for development

The first thing we need to do is install a local Redash for the development process.

There are two options to do this:

- Use a Docker-based development environment
- Use a regular development environment
- Connect to a remote server while running the frontend locally

Installing a Docker-based developer environment

This type of installation relies on Docker (also known as a container, a computer program that performs OS-level virtualization).

Docker will be used to run all the services needed for Redash, except for Node.js, which will be running locally.

First, you will have to install Docker and Docker Compose. Details can be found at the following link: `https://docs.docker.com/install/#server`.

Afterwards, you must install Node.js (`https://nodejs.org/en/download/`).

When Docker, Docker Compose, and Node.js are installed, we can get to Redash itself.

 This type of installation is recommended for newcomers to Redash and beginner developers.

Initial dev setup

- Obtain the Redash source code by cloning the repository, and enter the Redash directory (very important):

```
git clone git@github.com:getredash/redash.git
cd redash/
```

- After cloning Redash and entering the Redash directory, you need to create the Docker services:

```
docker-compose up
```

This will build the Docker images and fetch some pre-built images before starting the services that are necessary for Redash operations (Redash web server, celery workers, PostgreSQL, and the Redis Key-Value store). You can refer to the `docker-compose.yml` file (if located under the Redash root directory) to see the full configuration of Docker-related services.

- Install the npm packages (npm is the default package manager for the JavaScript runtime environment Node.js):

```
npm install
```

- Create the Redash Operational Database. First of all, you will need to create the tables, as follows:

```
docker-compose run --rm server create_db
```

- And then, create the database for tests:

```
docker-compose run --rm postgres psql -h postgres -U postgres -c
    "create database tests"
```

Dev use

To start all Docker services, you have two options: you can use either `docker-compose up` or `docker-compose start`.

Once all Docker services are running, you can validate this by verifying that Redash is available at `http://localhost:5000/`.

We will use the webpack dev server (`https://webpack.js.org/configuration/dev-server/`) here. However, we still need to build the frontend assets at least once, as some of them are used for static pages (for example, the login page). To do this, run the following code:

```
npm run build
```

To work on the frontend code, you will need the webpack dev server up and running:

```
npm run start
```

Now, the dev server will be available at `http://localhost:8080`, and you will be able to see the login screen for the first time:

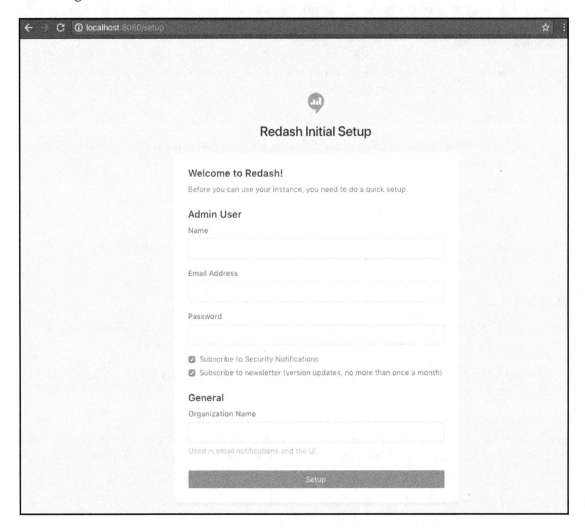

This rebuilds the frontend code every time you change it and refreshes the browser.

All the API calls are proxied to `localhost:5000` (the backend server running in Docker).

- **Restarting Celery Workers**: The web server will restart on code changes, but the Celery workers won't. In case you need to restart them, for example when modifying a query runner's code, run the following command (or just stop `docker-compose up` and run it again):

```
docker-compose restart worker
```

- **Installing new Python packages** (`requirements.txt`): If you pulled a new version with new packages, or added packages by yourself, you will need to rebuild the server and worker images. You can do so by using the following commands:

```
docker-compose build worker
docker-compose build server
```

- Running tests:

```
docker-compose run --rm server tests
```

Before running tests for the first time, you need to create a database for the tests:

```
docker-compose run --rm postgres psql -h postgres -U postgres -c "create
database tests;"
```

Installing a regular developer environment

This type of installation is recommended for more experienced developers.

Installing dependencies

You must install Python, PostgreSQL, Redis, and Node.js before going any further.

Refer to the documentation of Python (2.7), PostgreSQL (9.3 or newer), Redis (2.8.3 or newer), and Node.js (v6 or newer) to learn more about how to install them in your environment. On macOS, you can use `brew` to install them. On Linux, you can use your package manager (`yum`/`apt-get`); just make sure it installs the aforementioned versions.

Installing the necessary Python packages

For development, the minimum required packages to install are described in the following files (located in the root directory of Redash):

- `requirements.txt`
- `requirements_dev.txt`

You can install them using `pip`:

```
pip install -r requirements.txt -r requirements_dev.txt
```

 In case Redash is not the only Python app on your development station, it's recommended that you use an environment manager such as `conda` or `virtualenv` when installing Python packages.

The basic requirement files do not include all the data sources and their dependencies. Additional dependencies for data sources are located and installed from the `requirements_all_ds.txt` file, and Oracle-specific requirements are in `requirements_oracle_ds.txt`file.

Node.js packages and assets

You can install all of the necessary packages with the following code:

```
npm install
```

Before running Redash for the first time, you will need to build the UI assets with the following code:

```
npm run build
```

Redash configuration

For development, in most cases the default configuration is enough. However, if you need to adjust the database configuration, email settings, or any other setting (any of the settings described in `Chapter 2`, *Installing Redash*, under the *Redash environment settings* section), you do so with environment variables.

To avoid having to export these variables manually, you can use a `.env` file and the `bin/run` helper script. By invoking any command with the `bin/run` prefix, it will load your environment variables from the `.env` file and then run your command, for example:

```
bin/run ./manage.py check_settings
```

Creating Redash operational database tables

Those are the tables for Redash's operational and metadata DB (PostgreSQL):

```
bin/run ./manage.py database create_tables
```

Starting Redash's main processes

The main Redash processes you have to run are as follows:

- Web server
- Celery worker(s) and the scheduler

In development, you will also run Webpack's dev server (`https://webpack.js.org/configuration/dev-server/`) or watch utility.

Our recommendations are as follows:

- **Web server:** `bin/run ./manage.py runserver --debugger --reload`
- **Celery workers:** `./bin/run celery worker --app=redash.worker --beat -Qscheduled_queries,queries,celery -c2`
- **Webpack dev server:** `npm run start`

This will result in a Flask web server listening on port `5000`, the Webpack dev server on port `8080`, and two Celery workers ready to run queries.

To open the app in your web browser, use Webpack's dev server, `localhost:8080`, which will auto-reload and refresh whenever you make changes to the frontend code.

Running tests

Currently, there are only tests for the backend code. To run them, invoke the following code:

```
pytest tests/
```

Connecting to the remote server while running the frontend locally

If you only want to work on the frontend side of Redash, and have a Redash instance deployed already (running version 1.0.0 or later), you can use that instance as your API server and run the Webpack dev server locally.

This setup is the most useful when you need to create a new visualization or change a dashboard layout, and you want to use your existing data sources and queries when presenting it.

The setup in this case is much simpler than the previous ones:

1. Install Node.js (`https://nodejs.org/en/download/`)
2. Obtain the Redash source code by cloning the repository, and enter the Redash directory (very important):

   ```
   git clone git@github.com:getredash/redash.git
   cd redash/
   ```

3. Install the `npm` packages by using the following code:

   ```
   npm install
   ```

4. Start the webpack dev server with the following code:

   ```
   REDASH_BACKEND="URL of your redash server" npm run start
   ```

The `REDASH_BACKEND` part of the command sets the URL of the remote Redash server you want to connect your local frontend to.

Summary

In this chapter, we covered cases where we need to extend Redash beyond what initially comes with the distribution, such as new data sources/visualizations/alerts or dashboard layouts. We also explained the two main options to extend Redash: the API, which allows us to call all of the Redash functionalities through HTTP calls, and the more comprehensive extension, by coding.

Regarding APIs, we reviewed all of the possible API calls, and regarding code, we covered the development setup options. Of course, the best source for understanding Redash is the source code.

The book ends here, but your journey to mastering Redash only begins here. The purpose of this book is to give you the tools to get started with Redash, along with querying and visualizing your data as quickly as possible. In addition, we cover all the other Redash possibilities such as Alerts, APIs, and Extension options in brief. Being an Open Source project, Redash allows everyone to customize it to meet their specific needs. Moreover, the source is the most powerful documentation possible.

Don't be scared to take a look at the code whenever you have advanced questions or when you think of a feature that might be very useful to your company.

We hope you find this book useful, and when combined with Redash features, you will be able to take data-driven decisions in your company to a whole new level.

Other Books You May Enjoy

If you enjoyed this book, you may be interested in these other books by Packt:

Mastering Qlik Sense

Martin Mahler, Juan Ignacio Vitantonio

ISBN: 9781783554027

- Understand the importance of self-service analytics and the IKEA-effect
- Explore all the available data modeling techniques and create efficient and optimized data models
- Master security rules and translate permission requirements into security rule logic
- Familiarize yourself with different types of **Master Key Item**(**MKI**) and know how and when to use MKI.
- Script and write sophisticated ETL code within Qlik Sense to facilitate all data modeling and data loading techniques
- Get an extensive overview of which APIs are available in Qlik Sense and how to take advantage of a technology with an API
- Develop basic mashup HTML pages and deploy successful mashup projects

Microsoft Power BI Quick Start Guide
Devin Knight

ISBN: 9781789138221

- Connect to data sources using both import and DirectQuery options
- Use the Query Editor to apply data transformations and data cleansing processes, including learning how to write M and R scripts
- Design optimized data models by designing relationships and DAX calculations
- Leverage built-in and custom visuals to design effective reports
- Use the Power BI Desktop and Power BI Service to implement Row Level Security on your model
- Administer a Power BI cloud tenant for your organization
- Deploy your Power BI Desktop files into the Power BI Report Server

Leave a review - let other readers know what you think

Please share your thoughts on this book with others by leaving a review on the site that you bought it from. If you purchased the book from Amazon, please leave us an honest review on this book's Amazon page. This is vital so that other potential readers can see and use your unbiased opinion to make purchasing decisions, we can understand what our customers think about our products, and our authors can see your feedback on the title that they have worked with Packt to create. It will only take a few minutes of your time, but is valuable to other potential customers, our authors, and Packt. Thank you!

Index

U

Url
  connecting to 91
user-defined function (UDF) 98
users
  creating 54, 55

V

visualizations types
  boxplot 141
  chart 142
  Choropleth map 145
  Cohort 146
  counter 146
  funnel 147
  Markers map 147
  pivot table 148
  Sankey chart type 150
  sunburst sequence 151
  table 152
  word cloud 152
visualizations
  actions 171
  benefits 139
  creating 68, 69, 70, 72, 73
  editing 154
  Redash visualizations 156
  types 141
  using 153

W

Webpack's dev server
  reference 197, 201

Y

Yandex
  reference 79

www.ingramcontent.com/pod-product-compliance
Lightning Source LLC
LaVergne TN
LVHW081523050326
832903LV00025B/1613

* 9 7 8 1 7 8 8 9 9 6 1 6 7 *